Oxford Socio-Legal Studies

Wills, Inheritance, and Families

OXFORD SOCIO-LEGAL STUDIES

Oxford Socio-Legal Studies is a series of books exploring the role of law in society for both an academic and a wider readership. The series publishes theoretical and empirically-informed work, from the United Kingdom and elsewhere, by social scientists and lawyers which advances understanding of the social reality of law and legal processes.

WILLS, INHERITANCE, AND FAMILIES

JANET FINCH, LYNN HAYES, JENNIFER MASON,
JUDITH MASSON, AND LORRAINE WALLIS

CLARENDON PRESS . OXFORD
1996

Oxford University Press, Walton Street, Oxford OX2 6DP
Oxford New York
Athens Auckland Bangkok Bombay
Calcutta Cape Town Dar es Salaam Delhi
Florence Hong Kong Istanbul Karachi
Kuala Lumpur Madras Madrid Melbourne
Mexico City Nairobi Paris Singapore
Taipei Tokyo Toronto
and associated companies in
Berlin Ibadan

Oxford is a trade mark of Oxford University Press

Published in the United States
by Oxford University Press Inc., New York

British Library Cataloguing in Publication Data
Data available

Library of Congress Cataloging in Publication Data
Wills, inheritance, and families / Janet Finch . . . [et al.].
p. cm.–(Oxford socio-legal studies)
Includes bibliographical references.
1. Wills—Great Britain. 2. Inheritance and succession—Great Britain. 3. Domestic relations—Great Britain. I. Finch, Janet. II. Series.
KD1509.W545 1995
346.7305'2—dc20
[347.30652] 95–40592

ISBN 0-19-8258348
1 3 5 7 9 10 8 6 4 2

Typeset by J&L Composition Ltd., Filey, North Yorkshire
Printed in Great Britain on acid-free paper by
Bookcraft Ltd., Midsomer Norton, Avon

General Editor's Introduction

Most people do not make a will. But for those who do, the will represents a series of personal decisions that may have profound consequences. It is a means by which private wishes about the disposal of property are transmitted to take effect after death, though the private wishes embodied in the will become public and legally enforceable. In a society based on the private ownership of property, the authors of this book argue, a document which disposes of property after death assumes considerable social and economic importance. While inheritance is central to the distribution of wealth, its significance has shifted over time. In recent years it has acquired greater importance with increasing levels of, and changing patterns in, home and property ownership. Patterns of inheritance are also affected by changing social conditions—shifts in the birth rate, in life expectancy, in rates of marriage and divorce, and so on. Inheritance may now be more relevant to larger numbers of people, while the family circumstances within which it occurs become increasingly varied.

The will is an important social document, then, one that is a rich source of social data about the testator's intentions, and family and other private relationships, a publicly available statement, as it were, about private relationships. But it is a document that seems to have been explored little, if at all, by socio-legal scholars, many of whom have worked extensively on problems of the family, while neglecting the matter of inheritance. *Wills, Inheritance and the Family*, with its empirical analysis of a large, randomly-selected sample of wills, thereby opens up a new terrain of socio-legal enquiry. This is not simply a book for those lawyers interested in wills and inheritance, but it is one which should be studied by those concerned with questions of social policy. Indeed, its empirical basis should grant it a wider readership among those interested in demographic change and in redistributive questions, as well as in the sociology of the family.

Keith Hawkins

Preface and acknowledgements

This book is the product of collaboration between five members of a research team who were funded by the Economic and Social Research Council to undertake a project on Inheritance, Property and Family Relationships (R00232035). We acknowledge with gratitude the support of the ESRC for a project which comprised three different components. One of these was an analysis of a random sample of 800 probated wills; data from this study form the basis of discussion in chapters 3, 4, 5 and 6 of this book.

The project was based at Lancaster University and the team comprised, as directors, Janet Finch (now Vice Chancellor of Keele University), Jennifer Mason (now Senior Lecturer in Sociology at Leeds) and Judith Masson (Professor of Law at Warwick University); the research associates were Lynn Hayes and Lorraine Wallis (the latter now in the Department of Adult Continuing Education at Leeds University).

The authors would like to thank a number of people whose advice and support has assisted the production of the book. The statistical analysis of the data was assisted in Lancaster by the unstinting support of Brian Francis and in Warwick by Professor John Copas and Dr Robin Reed. The processing and production of data was assisted in Warwick by Moyra Butterworth and in Lancaster by Pam Holme, who was secretary to the Inheritance Project and whose support was a significant contribution to its success. Helen Beresford gave assistance with the typing of early drafts and Sandra Irving produced revised and final versions of the manuscript in her characteristically careful and efficient way. The authors would like to convey their warm thanks to all of these.

Contents

1 Wills As Social Documents

Why study wills?

This book is about wills, in particular what they can tell us about the ways in which inheritance is used in contemporary Britain, especially in the context of family relationships. In this introductory chapter we shall consider the question: what are the distinctive characteristics of contemporary wills, as a resource for social research? Exploring this question highlights the value of studying wills as social documents, and also helps to identify their limitations. In the course of this introduction we shall also give details of our own study of 800 wills, on which this book draws.

A will is a written document which represents a unique form of communication between the dead and the living. Textbooks on the law tend to make the conventional but important distinction between two different meanings of the word 'will'. First, there is what someone 'wills' in a metaphysical sense; second, there is the physical document which expresses these wishes in a prescribed form, known as 'a will' (Mellows, 1983: 6–7). A 'will' in the latter sense is a form of communication between someone who has died and others who survive. It is principally associated with the deceased person's wishes about who should claim ownership of his or her property. That 'property' can range from assets which are very valuable in monetary terms to items which are simply of personal or symbolic significance. A will can be made by any adult of sound mind, however modest their assets. It is a statement of wishes which only comes into effect—literally, only becomes a will—after its author has died. Before that date any will is always provisional, since it can be revoked and a new will written, or it can be amended by the addition of a codicil. After a death the validity of a will must be proved in the court of probate before its provisions can take effect, unless it concerns a small estate whose size and the types of property included make it exempt under the Administration of Estates Act 1965.

The uniqueness of a will derives not simply from the fact that it is a way of influencing what happens after one's own death, or even the fact that this is done in the form of a written document. There are other ways in which people sometimes try to influence or control those who live after them, including through other types of written documents such as letters or papers. The uniqueness of a will lies in the fact that, provided it is produced in the prescribed way, it becomes a public document once probated and carries the force of law. Thus a statement of the intentions of a dead person, which constitute a personal statement of that individual's wishes, will be supported in the public arena, and enforced by the courts if necessary. A will is therefore both a private and a public document. This chapter explores further some of the distinctive consequences which flow from that as well as introducing our own study of 800 wills which is used in later chapters.

In order to be recognised as a 'will' which has legal force, the statement of the wishes of the individual writing it—the testator[1]—must be produced in a form prescribed under the current law of a particular jurisdiction. For England and Wales this is the Wills Act 1837, as modified by subsequent legislation and most recently by the Administration of Justice Act 1982 (Law Reform Committee, 1980; Mellows, 1983). We explain the details of this in chapter 3. Though normally associated with the transmission of property from the dead to the living, a will may also cover other matters such as the disposal of the testator's body by burial or cremation, or arrangements for the guardianship of children. Indeed a document which concerns only these matters, and does not mention property, will be recognised as a will provided it is made in the prescribed form (Mellows, 1983: 6–7). A will may be drawn up with advice from a professional, but this is not a requirement.

As a mechanism for transmitting property from one person to another, and from one generation to the next over time, wills are of considerable social and economic significance. Of course they are not the only means by which such transmissions can be accomplished. Transfers can be made between one generation and the next during the lifetime of an older person, either as part of the process of setting up the younger generation in adult life (for example, substantial gifts at the time of a marriage) or in anticipation of death, when it may be advantageous for tax purposes to make the transfer before the death occurs. There are therefore various different methods available—of

[1] Throughout the book we use the word 'testator' though strictly this refers to a man. However, the female form 'testatrix' is less commonly used in normal speech and less widely understood. We intend therefore that the word 'testator' should be taken as gender neutral. Where referring to either men alone or women alone, we make that clear in the text.

which a will is just one—to secure the transfer of property in a way which enables the person who owns it to retain control over its disposal. Indeed it can be argued that the wealthy have always used these different methods in a flexible manner, to ensure maximum benefit particularly to their own children and grandchildren (Scott, 1982: 119). Within this broader picture, the transfer of property after a death represents the final settlement of that property on the next generation, or their final exclusion from it, if the testator has chosen to will his or her property to friends or to charity, for example.

The transfer of property will take place after a death, whether or not the deceased made a valid will. This is an important point because many people do not leave a will and only a minority of the population makes a will which is admitted to probate. Where this has not happened, disposal of the property will occur under the laws governing intestacy, which do place descendent generations of the deceased's own family in a privileged position. So the whole process of inheritance—whether accomplished through a will or under intestacy—is centrally concerned with the transmission of property down the generations. What a will tells us distinctively is how individuals choose to dispose of their property when they do exercise their right to make their own decisions about this. This is of particular interest under those jurisdictions, England included, which allow testators considerable freedom to dispose of their property as they wish. We shall return to this point in chapter 2.

In a society based upon the private ownership of property—land, businesses, capital, stocks, and shares—these arrangements for its transmission over time are of central importance in reproducing the social and economic order. In that sense, it is difficult to overestimate the importance of inheritance, in which wills play a central role. Many writers have recognised its particular significance in linking economic and personal relationships, perhaps most famously Friedrich Engels who saw inheritance as a driving force in the formation of different types of family throughout history. He was particularly critical of the effects of arrangements for the ownership of private property, and its transmission through inheritance, in nineteenth-century Britain. These arrangements, he argued, had led to a form of marriage amongst the bourgeois classes which was dominated by concerns about property and its transmission from father to son, leaving women as little more than unpaid prostitutes, needed because their bodies were necessary to produce sons but otherwise excluded from the process (Engels, 1985 edition: 101–3).

Though the evidence on which Engels based his analysis in many ways now appears flawed, few would dispute his central insight into the role of inheritance in reproducing privilege. The process of transferring property, either during the lifetime of both parties or through inheritance after a death, enables wealth to be retained within a very small group of families over time. This applies to the twentieth as much as to the nineteenth century despite some changes in the distribution of wealth. John Scott, a scholar working on the distribution of wealth in contemporary Britain, concludes that still no more than 1 per cent of the population owns a high proportion of national wealth. The exact proportion depends how 'wealth' is defined but there is a particularly clear concentration in respect of unearned income derived from income-generating assets (Scott, 1982: 116). Much of this unearned income is likely to have been inherited. Indeed about two-thirds of top wealth holders themselves have received a substantial inheritance. Thus Scott sees inheritance as playing a crucial role not simply in transmitting property over time, but in doing so in ways which highlight family relationships as crucial: 'what is brought out by [the foregoing] discussion is the continuing importance of the family in the perpetuation of economic privilege. Inheritance remains the major determinant of wealth inequality as well as the other life chances which depend on this.' (ibid: 119)

In addition to its continuing importance in the transmission of major economic assets within a wealthy minority of families, inheritance now has a new significance well beyond that privileged minority for whom it has always been important. The major reason for this is the spread of home ownership in the UK. In the thirty-year period between 1960 and 1990 the proportion of households living in owner-occupied property doubled, from one-third to two-thirds. Current predictions are that it will continue to rise to a level at which about three-quarters of homes are owned rather than rented (Hamnett, Harmer, and Williams, 1991). This is a social change with many economic and political consequences, among them the fact that many more people than in the past now have something substantial to bequeath, namely a house or its value when converted into monetary terms. To this we can add the opening up of the opportunity for women to own property once the Married Women's Property Act 1882 removed restrictions on the rights of married women over the ownership and disposal of property. Though certainly this did not make an immediate or dramatic difference in the gendered nature of property ownership, it opened up the legal means for married women to become owners. Concerns about the fragility of marriage, plus the increased economic activity of women, have made it more common for couples to own property jointly in recent decades (Eekelaar and Maclean, 1986). So we can say that the twentieth century has seen a much wider range of people brought into the sphere of property ownership, especially ownership of housing, and therefore—potentially—of inheritance. This would be particularly true of the last forty years.

Thus inheritance, which until the middle of the twentieth century could be seen as a matter which essentially concerned only a small minority of the population, is now rapidly becoming a matter for the majority, since by definition it is likely that most people (though not all) will have the experience of being either a testator or a beneficiary, or both, in a transfer of property which has a significant value. This represents a major change in the social significance of inheritance, and it cannot necessarily be assumed that these 'new inheritors' will wish to dispose of their property in exactly the same way as those whose families have had experience of inheritance across several generations. Indeed some evidence from the past suggests that we should expect significant changes when a new generation of property owners begins to write wills. In the early nineteenth century, when a generation of new entrepreneurs built up wealth based on industrial manufacturing, it appears that the new property owners of that period did choose to bequeath their property to the next generation in ways which were significantly different from the aristocratic families who had hitherto dominated the inheritance scene (Davidoff and Hall, 1987: 205–7). Under English law, especially from 1833 onwards, it was possible for people to make a range of choices for the disposition of their property, because of the priority accorded to the principle of testamentary freedom. We discuss the contemporary significance of this for the study of wills in chapter 2.

Inheritance therefore concerns more people than hitherto, and the effects of this on the kinds of wills which people write are not entirely predictable. We have no way of knowing, for example, whether it will become more common in the future than it is now for property to be transferred during the testator's lifetime, leaving a relatively small amount to be transmitted after death, or for people to make use of the equity invested in their property to finance their own support in old age (Kendig, 1984; Leather, 1990). Further complications arise as a result of demographic changes which mean, in brief, that the families from which contemporary testators come often have a different shape and composition from families in the past. Though there is no need to elaborate these changes in detail, some of the more important features need to be highlighted, since they form an essential context within which inheritance now needs to be understood.

First, changes in fertility mean that the number of children in each generation is likely to be smaller for cohorts born since the First World War than in previous cohorts. This means that, if property passes from one generation to the next within the family, there are fewer children to be considered than there were in the past. Second, the overlap between generations has changed significantly, because of a combination of increased life expectancy and the age at which children have been born to parents in the twentieth century. As a consequence an adult 'child', born in 1946 from a statistically typical family, can now expect to inherit from his or her parents at the age of 56. The equivalent age would have been 37 for someone born in 1891 (Anderson, 1985). Inheritance therefore, as Anderson has pointed out, now passes assets to the next generation at a point well beyond any which could make a difference to launching that generation into adult life. Third, increased rates of divorce and remarriage, especially since the early 1970s, mean that many more families than in the past are likely to have members with complicated step-relationships, commitments to children of more than one marriage, and possibly a continuing financial relationship with a former spouse (Kiernan, 1989). Clearly the effects of this are likely to be to more complex patterns of bequeathing though in ways that are—as yet—little understood. Finally, in the second half of the twentieth century Britain has become established as a multi-racial society, with substantial numbers of citizens being of South East Asian or African–Caribbean descent. Amongst those of Asian descent in particular there is a high rate of home ownership (*Social Trends*, 1993, Table 8.23). Though of course they are subject to the limitations of English or Scottish law, such citizens may have expectations about inheritance drawn from different cultural traditions, and it is open to them to use the mechanism of a will to ensure that such expectations are activated. Ultimately this may have the effect of making patterns of bequeathing in the UK more diverse, though little is known about this at the present time.

We would argue therefore that inheritance in general, and wills in particular, repay serious study for several reasons. Inheritance following a death has always been an important topic because of its central role in the transmission of wealth over time. It is of particular importance in sustaining the central role of the family in control over wealth. It offers one particular perspective on family and kin relationships, and the role of money in underpinning them in those families who hold significant economic assets (Finch, 1989: 17–20). However, the social and economic conditions of late twentieth-century Britain mean that inheritance is of relevance to many more families than in the past, whilst at the same time the family circumstances within which it occurs are in many ways more diverse.

A study of wills offers one perspective on inheritance in the contemporary world, by showing what people choose to do when they exercise their right to determine the disposition of their own property. It enables us to explore how people might conceptualize the claims of different individuals upon them, in the context of their own family circumstances and in the light of public expectations about such claims. This is possible because a will is at the same time both a private and a public document. It is 'private' in that it is an entirely individual and personal statement of the wishes of the testator in respect of his or her own family and friends. On the other hand, it can only be a valid will if it conforms to public expectations about the form which such documents should take. Further, though the testator may have kept its contents entirely secret during his or her lifetime, and indeed may have changed it several times, after death the probated will becomes a document in the public domain, and must necessarily be so if it is to have effect. It is this unique character of a will as both a private and a public document which leads us to characterize it as a distinctive means of communication between the dead and the living.

Wills as documentary data

Wills therefore represent a publicly available resource for research and, we have argued, there are good reasons for using them as one way of understanding inheritance in the context of family relationships. Whilst wills have long been a standard source of data for historians, social scientists studying the contemporary world have made rather little use of them. The main focus has been on inheritance as a vehicle for transmitting significant wealth and, where use has been made of wills, it has largely been by a small number of scholars who have tended to focus on estate size rather than other features of the will (Harbury, 1962; Harbury and Hitchins, 1979; Hamnett, Harmer, and Williams, 1991).

These studies notwithstanding, in general it appears that wills represent a surprisingly under-exploited resource in social research. Though this observation perhaps applies in general to written documents, wills would appear to be a particularly neglected resource. Even a rare, specific (and admirably wide-ranging) text on documentary data does not identify wills as an example of written documents available for research (Scott, 1990). However, if—as we are arguing—wills represent a potential resource for social research, we need to think carefully about their status as data. In doing so we can generate further substantive insights into the nature of wills as both private and public documents.

It is common ground amongst the most recent authorities that, when written documents are used as the basis for empirical research, they should be subject to the same rigorous criteria as other types of research data (Platt, 1981; Scott, 1990). We concur with that view. One distinctive feature of much documentary data, wills included, is that the data come in a form which is already 'fixed' before the researcher gets access to it unlike the product of interviews, for example, where the researcher has direct input into the creation of the data in a particular form (Scott, 1990: 4). It follows therefore that researchers who use documentary data must take considerable care to understand the context in which these data were created, and their purpose as intended by those who participated in the production of the documents.

To assist researchers' thinking about the types of documents which they are using, Scott (1990: 13–18) has produced a useful classification. Though wills do not fit this classification with complete ease, it is nonetheless a helpful way of thinking about their distinctive character as social documents. Scott's classification works with two dimensions: authorship and access. By 'authorship' Scott refers to the origins of the documents, to the 'hand' which wrote them or on whose behalf they were issued. He makes a distinction here between 'personal' and 'public' documents, and further subdivides public documents into those issued on behalf of state bureaucracies and those issued by private organisations. The dimension of 'access' refers to the readership rather than the authorship of the documents: who may have access to them? He has four categories here, from the completely closed to the completely open and widely published.

In thinking about how wills fit into this classification, one comes up against some problems which themselves serve to highlight the distinctive nature of a will. Essentially the distinction between 'personal' and 'official' documents does not fit wills, since they are both. They are clearly personal documents, in the sense that the author is a single individual, not an organisation. Also they refer to personal rather than public affairs. However, a document only 'counts' as a will if it is drawn up in accordance with publicly endorsed criteria, which may act as a constraint on individual intentions. It also must be done in a way which is semi-public, in the sense that it must involve witnesses. Furthermore, it takes effect only once it is proved and has become a document in the public domain. This adds another complexity. There is a sense in which 'last' wills (the subject of our own study) have an especially public dimension in that anyone may obtain a copy. Earlier wills, which subsequently may be superseded, also have a public dimension in that they must be drawn up according to public criteria and be witnessed; but they can remain private in the sense that only those involved in drawing them up may ever know of their contents.

Building on Scott's categories, we would therefore argue that a will is *both* a private and a public document, in a strong sense. We are not saying that it is a document some way 'between' the categories of personal and official. Rather, it is both of these at one and the same time, though its public or official aspects become more prominent after its author's death. Similarly its status on the dimension of 'access' changes over time. When a will is made, and up to the time its author dies, access to it is completely 'closed' (though of course the testator may choose to show it to certain individuals). When its author dies, and the will is proved as a valid will, it becomes a public document with what Scott calls 'open-archival' access. That is, it becomes one of a class of documents which is stored in public archives, where researchers and members of the general public may use it subject to only minimal administrative restrictions (Scott, 1990: 14). In fact, once proved, wills are stored in the Public Records Office, from where we drew our own sample. A will therefore is a distinctive type of social document, in that it is at the same time both personal and official, and in that it changes its status over time from closed to open access.

This distinctive status as a public–private document has many ramifications. Once in the official domain, a will becomes a publicly available statement about an individual's private relationships. It tells us whom a testator wished to acknowledge by leaving a bequest (though of course it tells us nothing about any people who have been excluded from bequests except unusually; we discuss this further in chapter 4). It tells us the types of bequests which a testator thought appropriate to leave to different individuals: cash, a house, items of personal property, shares, land, or simply a proportion of his or her estate. If the total or residuary estate is divided proportionately, it tells us what proportions the testator thought fit to leave to different individuals through the mechanism of a will. All of this is of considerable interest under a jurisdiction, such as English law, which leaves testators essentially free to make their own decisions about the disposition of their property (see chapter 2).

In a sense therefore a will is a document which lays open to public inspection aspects of the pattern of relationships which a testator had with members of his or her family, and with other people. Occasionally, the reasons for different forms of bequest, and the relationships which lie behind them, are spelled out in the will. Some examples of such wills, drawn from our own study, are quoted in later chapters. More commonly, the testator does not spell out reasons for different forms of distribution, and one of the challenges for a researcher using wills is to be able to see behind these patterns without interpreting them in an unjustifiable way. In respect of any single will therefore, interpreting the testator's motivation has to be approached with caution.

However, if we take a large number of wills, what we can see is whether a common pattern emerges. This is the way in which Davidoff and Hall (1987) used a sample of 622 wills, from the late eighteenth and early nineteenth centuries, as one data source in their important study of the emergence of the English middle classes in the period 1780–1850. They are able to show that the emerging middle classes, who were crucial in establishing the new social and economic structures of industrial capitalism, bequeathed their assets in ways which were different from the aristocratic traditions and which fitted with their distinctive values and priorities. The key difference was that they moved away rapidly from the custom of primogeniture, which in aristocratic circles had been used to keep estates intact, transmitting them to one child, usually the eldest son. Instead the emerging middle classes were much more likely to write wills which distributed their assets on the basis of equality between their children and also often included a surviving spouse. Daughters as well as sons were quite likely to be included in these wills. Davidoff and Hall see some evidence that male testators attempted to give sons and daughters bequests of equal value, though usually in a different form, with daughters likely to have gifts in the form of trusts which provided them with income, whilst sons got land, property or liquid assets (ibid: 205–6). Of course these gendered distinctions in part reflect the fact that, in the period which that study covered, once daughters married they would not have been able to own property in their own right.

Though Davidoff and Hall do provide an interpretation of why the emerging middle classes used their wills in this way, data of this kind can be useful even if we cannot necessarily impute motives to the authors of wills. Where a common pattern like this emerges, its effects are significant whatever motives lay behind it. A single will can be seen as a public statement of one person's private relationships, which we may or may not be able to interpret with any degree of accuracy. A large collection of wills which show a common pattern is a sociologically significant statement about the kinds of relationships which people acknowledge as having claim on their resources, whether or not we can be certain of individual motives and rationales. They also give access to the interplay between private relationships and the legal and cultural contexts in which they are embedded. Thus a sample of wills, appropriately analysed, can give us access to collective understanding of claims, the ways they are formally expressed and handled, and how they can change over time.

Wills are, in essence, a potentially useful resource for social research if handled carefully. Their distinctive character, and their particular value to researchers, lies in the fact that they are a publicly available statement of relationships which otherwise are treated as private. Since family members figure prominently as beneficiaries, they offer an opportunity for insights into family and kin relationships, in particular those aspects which concern the transmission of items of monetary or personal value. Since kin relationships in the British context are generally quite fluid, and do not operate on the basis of fixed, public norms about how kin should be treated (Finch, 1989; Finch and Mason, 1993), there is particular interest in what wills can show about the way people acknowledge these relationships in reality.

The study of 800 wills

The data on which we draw in later chapters of this book come from a study of 800 probated wills. We used these wills to pursue the type of issues identified earlier in this chapter, concerning patterns of bequeathing and, particularly, the range of family and non-family claims which people acknowledge. We shall introduce this study here, leaving more detailed discussion of how the data were used to later chapters.

The 800 wills were sampled from Probate Calendars held at Somerset House. The Calendars give the testator's address at the time of death, the date of death, the date and place of probate, and, for the majority of estates sampled, the value of the estate.[2] We drew a random sample, which was possible because the Calendar for each year lists the surnames of the deceased alphabetically. We used random number tables to identify the estates to be included in our sample.

Before the sample was drawn, we stratified it in two ways: by year and by region. We sampled 200 from each of the following years: 1959, 1969, 1979,1989. The reason for drawing the sample over this period of time was to enable us to investigate whether there have been any clear changes in patterns of bequeathing over the period when more people have been drawn into home ownership. Information about the testator's address at the time of death enabled us to stratify the sample by region. Half of our sample were wills of people who had died in the south-east of England and half in the north-west. For three-quarters of our sample (607 wills) the address at the time of death was the same as that which appeared on the will. Our reason for building in this regional comparison was to ensure that we would pick up any variation in patterns of bequeathing consequent upon the higher value of houses in the south-east region; the north-west was selected as a comparator because a separate interview study (not reported in this book) was taking place in this region.

Is 800 an appropriate sample size for the type of analysis which we are undertaking? Though the size of any sample must always be a compromise between the ideal and the practically achievable, we believe that reasonable confidence can be placed on the sample, for most of the purposes for which we are using it. It compares with the 1,000 wills used by Hamnett, Harmer, and Williams (1991) in the other recent study to use this data source. Moreover, whilst it would have yielded an inadequate number had we wished to focus on large estates

[2] From August 1981 there were changes in the way in which estate values were recorded in the Calendars (Hamnett, Harmer, and Williams, 1991: 85). From that date, it became unusual for the precise value of the estate to be recorded, especially for smaller estates. Instead the following categories were introduced: not exceeding £40,000, not exceeding £70,000, and not exceeding £100,000.

(Munro, 1988), our explicit intention was to study the wills of testators from 'ordinary' families.

From a statistical standpoint, in social science there is never an absolute answer to the question of how large a sample should be. It depends on the purposes for which the data are to be used and the circumstances in which they are collected (Bryman and Cramer, 1990: 98–104). For example, the prospect of non-response is a major issue in many cases but simply did not arise for us since, once sampled, we had access to 100 per cent of the documents which we had chosen. In relation to the purposes of our analysis, our principal aim was to produce descriptive statistics about patterns of bequeathing rather than to engage in complex statistical procedures to determine causal patterns.

In the course of our analysis we were able to construct a number of variables from the information available to us. The Probate Calendars, from which the sample was drawn, enabled us to identify a range of characteristics about the testators in our sample which could be used in the analysis: gender, region, estate size, date of death. To this we added information about the testator's age at the time of death. We took this information from death certificates by the following means. The information in the Probate Calendars was used to locate entries in the register of deaths, which are also public documents held at St. Catherine's House. The register for 1959 gives the actual age at death. This is not so for our other sample years but, since the date of birth is given, it was a simple matter to calculate the age at death. We succeeded in getting this information for 720 of our testators. For the remaining 80, the information given was insufficient to link the will and the death certificate with complete confidence, usually because the testator had a rather common name.

Thus we were able to construct a number of variables concerning the characteristics of testators and their circumstances from the registers. In addition the inclusion of four sample years enabled us to construct a measure of change over time, though this proved a complex issue and is worth explaining in some detail. The fundamental problem concerns the randomness, in a statistical sense, of the measures of time available to us. Our sample of wills is representative of the wills probated in four sample years. However, the wills probated in those years may have been written at any point up to and including the year in which they were probated. Therefore our sample is *not* randomly selected in relation to the year in which the will was *written*. This is a problem for measuring changes over time, since we are interested precisely in testators' intentions when they wrote their wills. In this analysis therefore we can not use the year in which the will was written because we have not randomly sampled for this.

In order to address these problems, we have created a time-variable which combines the time at which the will was written with the gap between when the person wrote the will and when s/he died. In doing this the effect is to limit ourselves to looking at the wills probated in our four sample years which were also written in the previous nine years; for example, wills probated in 1989 which were written between 1980 and 1989. Though resolving the statistical problems of creating an appropriate measure of change over time, this approach nonetheless has other consequences which we need to take into account in our interpretations of the data. Since, on average, three-quarters of wills are written within nine years of death, this time-variable is representative of 75 per cent of wills written in this time period. However, as our analysis in chapter 4 shows, testators over 75 are far more likely to die with an up-to-date will than are people who die younger. This means that people aged over 75 are more likely to be included in our analyses which use the time-variable. By the same token, testators who were not married at the time of writing their will are more likely to be included.

Other variables were constructed from the wills themselves. In most cases we were able to tell quite easily whether the will had been drawn up with the assistance of a solicitor or other professional adviser, from features such as the way in which witnesses identified themselves. On this basis, we classified 81.5 per cent of wills as professionally written, and 18.5 per cent as home-made.

Another important variable constructed from the wills themselves was the marital status of the testator at the time the will was written. A female testator seems often to be described by marital status in her will if she is a widow or a spinster, though her male counterparts are not normally so described. In the cases of such women, marital status is unambiguous; in other cases, one needs to look for clues in the will itself. For example, since many women take their husband's name after marriage, a woman's surname can be compared with that of siblings named in the will, particularly brothers, to assess whether a woman has been married. Requests to be buried alongside a former spouse can be taken to indicate widowhood. In common with other studies (Munro, 1988; Hamnett, Harmer, and Williams, 1991) we categorised as 'currently married' those testators who bequeathed to a spouse, unless there was some specific indication in the will that the marriage had ended.

Working on information of this type, we were able to categorise the marital status of most of our testators. Our coding frame kept separate those cases where we were confident of the marital status from those where this information was presumed on slightly less certain grounds. Only 48 wills gave no real clues about marital status; 67 per cent of wills allowed us to categorise a 'known' marital status and 28 per cent a 'presumed' one.

There are other characteristics of testators which it would be useful to know, but which could not be gleaned from the various sources of information available to us. Ethnic origins might be highly relevant to patterns of bequeathing, but in very few cases do wills offer any clues about this. Surnames are the most likely indicators, but even here it is difficult to interpret the information with any confidence. For example, a Polish surname could denote either a recent immigrant or a second generation descendant of a migrant, for whom 'Polishness' has little personal meaning. Conversely, a name which 'sounds' British could belong to a testator born, for example in the Caribbean. Further, for a married woman, a surname may show the ethnic origin of her spouse but be misleading about her own. We have therefore not attempted to use the factor of ethnicity in our analysis.

Social class is the other obvious variable on which one might wish to have information. However, if one takes an occupational definition of class, wills do not really afford the basis for categorising testators. Very few wills mention occupation. Even where they do, it is difficult to decide how to use that information since it would refer simply to the testator's occupation at the time the will was written, which might give a distorted picture of the position over his or her lifetime. The complexities of determining the social class of women from occupational data further compound the problem. In our sample therefore, the only accessible indicator of class position is the size of the estate—an indicator of wealth rather than occupational class, but obviously one which bears directly on the issue of bequeathing.

These then are the characteristics of testators and their circumstances which inform our analysis. They form one section of a fairly complex coding frame developed to aid our analysis. The coding frame was designed principally to enable us to explore our main substantive focus, namely patterns of bequeathing contained in the wills. It was divided into seven main sections:

1. Testator characteristics.
2. Information relating to executors.
3. Details of the overall patterns of first choice beneficiaries and bequests.
4. Details of first substitute beneficiaries and bequests.
5. Details of beneficiaries and bequests featured at the second and subsequent levels of substitution.
6. Information on each individual beneficiary (or group of beneficiaries) mentioned in the will, including their characteristics, types of bequest(s) received, conditions attached to each bequest, and status of beneficiary (i.e. whether first choice or substitute).
7. Details of people who are mentioned in the will but who do not receive a gift of any kind.

Information from all of these sections is made use of in our discussion in subsequent chapters. Data contained in the wills were extracted, coded, and analysed using SPSSX version 4. The main tests which were used were Pearsons Chi-square tests (for cross-tabulation of categorical data). Throughout this book, where a 'statistically significant difference' has been reported, this difference was found at a confidence level of at least 95 per cent (i.e. was significant at the level of less than 0.05).

How does the information thus gleaned measure up to generally accepted criteria for good quality documentary data? Is it reasonable to develop an analysis on the basis of these data with confidence that it is meaningful? In considering these issues, we refer to Scott's discussion in which he develops criteria for determining the quality of documentary data (Scott, 1990: 19–35). He argues that four tests can be applied:

1. Authenticity. Is the evidence genuine and of unquestionable origin?
2. Credibility. Is the evidence free from error and distortion?
3. Representativeness. Is the evidence typical of its kind and, if not, is the extent of the untypicality known?
4. Meaning. Is the evidence clear and comprehensible?

In relation to the first criterion, authenticity, our wills are very reliable as authenticated documents. They have been legally attested in the process of probate, a process designed *inter alia* to establish the authorship of the will. However, the position in relation to the criterion of credibility is less straightforward. As legal documents, wills are perhaps less open to the problem of error than many other types of document. On the other hand, some of our wills have been drawn up with the assistance of professional advisers, usually a solicitor, and thus it is possible that they reflect the solicitor's views on appropriate patterns of bequeathing rather more than the testator's. If we were to overlook this possibility and to interpret all the patterns which we discern in wills as the unmediated wishes of the testator, this might indeed lead to 'distortion', one of Scott's touchstones of the credibility of evidence. However, whether or not one calls this the possibility of 'distortion' or simply an issue about the *meaning* attributed to data from wills, is really a matter of the type of analysis being undertaken. Our discussion is live to this issue, and subsequent chapters return to it.

In relation to the criterion of representativeness, this is really a matter of how the sample was selected. As we have indicated, we were fortunate in being able to make use of a sampling frame suitable for constructing a random sample. Therefore on Scott's first three criteria we believe that our wills sample constitutes high quality documentary data, provided it is handled with due respect.

However, Scott's fourth criterion, meaning, is the area where particular care needs to be exercised if the reliability of these data is to be sustained. The issue here really concerns the purpose for which we are using data from the wills. As legal documents, all our wills have a meaning which can be seen as 'technical'. If any were challenged, the courts would determine its meaning, using established rules of interpretation. Our analysis has not been concerned directly with this 'technical' interpretation, which is designed to settle the outcome in practice. Our interest is in the more 'personal' meaning of the will for the testator at the time it was written, in particular what it reveals about his or her concepts of priorities in bequeathing. In developing an analysis of this type, there is a temptation to go beyond the evidence provided in the will in the assumptions which one makes about the testator's intentions. We have sought to resist this temptation firmly and, as we explained above, we would argue that more confidence can be placed in patterns discerned in the wills sample as a whole than we would place in our ability to interpret intentions in an individual will. We believe therefore that the quality of our data need not be compromised if we proceed in this way.

Research questions

We have used this chapter to review the use of wills as documents for use in social research. This has enabled us to identify a number of research questions which we shall follow through in subsequent chapters.

We have argued that inheritance is an important topic for study at the present time, and that wills give us one particular perspective on this topic. It is the perspective of those people who exercise their right to determine the disposition of their own property, rather than to have their estate dealt with under intestacy laws. The fact that English law gives considerable weight to the principle of testamentary freedom means that questions about how people choose to dispose of their property, by formal means, are more interesting and important than they would be under jurisdictions where testators are required to leave set proportions of their estate to relatives identified in law.

In this context, the special character of a will as both a private and a public document can be capitalised upon as a research resource. Such documents must be handled with the intellectual respect and care which should be accorded to all research data and there are, we have indicated, some specific areas where caution needs to be exercised in the interpretation of data of this type. Proceeding with due caution therefore, we can summarise the value of wills as social documents which give us access in a semi-public form to people's family relationships, in particular to those relationships which they wish to acknowledge with bequests of monetary or symbolic value. It can tell us much about whom and what is thus acknowledged when people have the choice, and whether there are in reality common ways of acknowledging certain types of relationship, even though the law does not require this.

The questions which we will take forward in the rest of the book therefore are:

1. What evidence can we glean about the process of will-making and how people approach it? Under what circumstances do people make wills? How common is it to take legal advice? How common is it for people to make changes to an existing will?
2. What does a sample of wills show us about people's concepts of 'family', as it relates to claims on inheritance? Is it clear that family members are the people to whom most gets bequeathed?

If so, how does the relevant membership of the 'family' get defined?

3. Is it possible to detect distributional principles in the ways in which estates get divided between different individuals? How prominent do principles such as equity and fairness seem to be? If apparently divided unequally between different beneficiaries, is it possible to detect any principles here: inequality by family position, by generation, or by gender, for example?
4. Can changes over time be detected? As the social context within which inheritance operates is changing, are people writing different types of wills?
5. In relation to all of these, how far do people's actions coincide with what the law assumes? What is the role of the law and legal context in the process of bequeathing?

Before we move on to discuss these issues specifically in relation to our own data, in chapter 2 we consider the significance of wills in the total pattern of inheritance under English law, since this forms part of the essential background against which any data must be interpreted. Then in chapter 3 we look at will-making as a process, before moving to consider the content of wills, and what they tell us about inheritance and the family in particular, in chapters 4, 5 and 6. Chapter 7 draws together various strands and returns to many of the issues developed in this chapter.

2 Wills and the Transmission of Property Under English Law

This chapter develops further the theme that wills are public as well as private documents, considering them specifically in a legal context. The law creates the very concept of a will as the mechanism for the transmission of property. In addition, any system of law can influence the content of people's wills either by requiring them to bequeath their property in certain ways or by forbidding certain types of disposition. Understanding the legal context therefore is essential in any study which seeks to interpret and draw conclusions from the provisions contained in wills.

The fact that the law does play a part in regulating wills is an expression of the strong public interest in the apparently private act of bequeathing. As the means by which one generation determines the distribution of property to the next, people other than those directly concerned do have a stake in the arrangements made. There is a public interest in who actually gets ownership and control of land, houses, businesses, and money, especially if the value of these items is significant. There is also a public interest in the position of members of the testator's family who do not receive bequests, since they will have to find their economic means of survival in some other way. Thus the consequences of the collective actions of testators in disposing of their property have a significant effect upon the distribution of wealth, control, and power in any society. Further, there is a public interest in ensuring that these 'private' actions are undertaken through a process which is reliable and which can be expedited without too much difficulty or cost.

Since industrialisation, the actions of the state—including legislation—have become the principal means for the expression of public interest in private acts. In this chapter we consider the ways in which the law in England and Wales seeks—and where it does not seek—to regulate the content of wills. We also consider the legal context of inheritance more broadly. Wills are but one way in which property is transmitted from one generation to the next. Alternatively, it may pass through gifts made *inter vivos* i.e. during the lifetime of the testator, which themselves are subject to legal regulation. Further, when someone dies not having made a will, the laws on intestacy determine who shall inherit. Taking this broader perspective therefore can help us to identify the limitations of what wills can tell us about inheritance, as well as yielding further data on the assumptions built into the law.

Testamentary freedom

How does English law seek to regulate the content of wills? Fundamental to understanding this is the concept of testamentary freedom, which is of central importance to legislation on wills in the context of English law.[1] The basic principle of testamentary freedom is that each testator is free to dispose of his or her property entirely on the basis of individual choice. The testator alone decides how his or her estate is to be divided, and who will receive it, and the law upholds the right of each individual to do that, however eccentric these decisions may seem to other people. In its purest form it implies the absolute right of the individual over property, in death as well as in life. In reality the law places some restrictions on that right, as we indicate below. However, in essence, under English law the testator has considerable freedom to decide who shall receive bequests, and also what form those bequests shall take.

The testator's freedom to dispose of property at death as s/he thinks fit has distinguished the family property regime in England and Wales from that of civil law countries. The Civil Code (introduced in France in 1804 and subsequently adopted elsewhere in Europe) bases laws of inheritance more clearly on the idea that certain family members (especially children) have the right to an equitable share of the parents' property. The distinction between these two approaches remains important though in reality legal developments (Kahn-Freund, 1955: 285; Miller, 1977: 24) and current practices have reduced the gulf between these systems. Historically, testamentary freedom without restriction has been the exception rather than the rule even in England and Wales, existing if at all, only for a short period between 1833 when it became possible to override 'dower', the widow's right to a life interest in one-third of her husband's land, and the enactment of the Inheritance (Family Provision) Act 1938. For

[1] The issues of principle discussed here apply equally to Scottish law, but historically they have been resolved somewhat differently in that jurisdiction. The following discussion therefore is confined to English law, since the sample of wills used in later chapters was drawn from English regions.

married women the right was even more transient because they only acquired testamentary capacity in the Married Women's Property Act 1882. Under common law there were legal limits on disposition by will (for example, the law against perpetuities, which we discuss below) but in England, from the fourteenth century, disinheritance of children and all relatives, except the widow, was generally permitted and property could be divided unequally as the testator saw fit.

It is beyond the scope of this book to consider in detail the historical reasons for the distinctiveness of English law in relation to testamentary freedom. However, there may well be a sense in which it reflects certain distinctive features of English society. Viewing it from a legal perspective, Miller asserts that complete testamentary freedom 'can only exist under social and economic conditions based on highly individualistic notions about property' (Miller, 1977: 18). Interestingly, this fits with a broader historical analysis of the distinctive features of English society from the fourteenth century onwards, which have been characterised by the concept of individualism. Unlike much of the rest of Western Europe during this period (including Wales, Ireland, and Scotland), it can be argued that English society placed much less emphasis on the ties of kinship and community, and much more on independence and individuality (Macfarlane, 1978). There is then a certain consistency between the general orientation to individualism and the emphasis on testamentary freedom.

However, other commentators have offered a more pragmatic explanation, namely that the public interest is well served by the ways in which people do bequeath their property in practice. The argument here depends upon the view that it is in the interests of the society as a whole that family solidarity should be upheld, as a means of ensuring social stability. In this context, inheritance can be seen as one important means to achieve this end, in that it binds together different generations through a common material interest. If this is true, it follows that it is in the public interest for property to pass in an orderly fashion from parent to child, ensuring meanwhile that the needs of a surviving spouse are catered for. However, it is unnecessary, it can be argued, to place restrictions on testators if they exercise their testamentary freedom in a way which secures precisely this end, at least in the majority of cases. In such circumstances, legal intervention is superfluous. As one commentator has put it, sentiment rather than law has ensured that property remains within the family in England (Crane, 1957: 255).

This interpretation implies that legal intervention would become necessary only if testators started to bequeath their property outside the family on a large scale, at which point the law would need to step in to support the claims of close kin. That the law does tend to support such claims, testamentary freedom notwithstanding, can be discerned from various laws which do exist in the area of inheritance generally. For example, the courts have powers to interpret a will whose meaning is ambiguous, and where there are insufficient clues about what the testator really intended. In exercising these powers the courts make certain assumptions. For example, it is assumed that when the testator uses a word such as 'niece' s/he means blood relations and not affines (that is, niece-in-law). Similarly it is assumed that s/he means the people of the exact degree specified, so that 'niece' does not include 'great-niece' (Mellows, 1983: 133–8). The assumptions being made here are that most people would recognise the claims of blood relatives over affines (that is, relatives by marriage), and would regard the claims of kin in the first descendent generation as stronger than those in the second.

Thus English law does recognise the concept of claims on a testator's estate, based upon notions of family rights and the obligation of a testator to acknowledge them. But at present these claims are acknowledged specifically only at the margins of the law on inheritance, for example where a will is not clear and has to be interpreted. Legislation on family provision (discussed below) is another example. It seems quite plausible therefore to argue that testamentary freedom can remain the basic principle of the law on inheritance only so long as most people exercise that freedom in ways which are consistent with the public interest, however defined.

It is not surprising therefore to find that testamentary freedom has been described not only as a right, but also as a duty and a responsibility. The 'right' to choose the destination of one's property, it has been argued, is 'felt psychologically to constitute an essential element of power over property' (Friedman, 1966: 355). The view that the right to make a will should be exercised by all who have the capacity (Davies, 1983: 6) establishes testamentary freedom as a duty. This 'duty' is moral, not legal; where no will is made, the modern law of intestacy seeks to arrange the distribution the deceased would have chosen rather than punish the failure to make a will. A contrary view, that the right to testamentary freedom should include the right *not* to make a will (Fellows, Simon, and Rau, 1978: 323), is recognised in the consideration given to developing appropriate provisions on intestacy and their continued review.

The 'responsibility' entailed in testamentary freedom lies in the expectation that it will not be used carelessly and the belief that wills normally protect the family. However where that ceases to be the case, the law may be modified. For example, before the enactment of the Administration of Estates Act 1925 the rules of intestate succession relating to realty, which favoured inheritance by the eldest son, were considered unsatisfactory. The interests of the family were seen to be furthered, and not threatened, by a will which could ensure the best use of the property by making a different disposition. However subsequently reform of intestacy laws themselves altered the balance again, helping to change attitudes to will-making because the alternative no longer seemed disadvantageous (Miller, 1977: 16, 91) and thus to create a climate where new controls on testamentary freedom could be established.

Three separate sets of rules now limit a testator's freedom to choose who will benefit from his or her will: the Inheritance (Provision for Family and Dependants) Act 1975, the rule against perpetuities (as modified by the Perpetuities and Accumulations Act 1964), and the doctrine of mutual wills. We consider each in turn in the next section.

Limitations on testamentary freedom in current law

The Inheritance Acts

In the light of the foregoing discussion, it is interesting that the key restrictions on testamentary freedom introduced during the twentieth century have been intended specifically to protect the close family of the testator from the possibility of exclusion from the will. These are: the Inheritance (Family Provision) Act 1938 and the Inheritance (Provision for Family and Dependants) Act 1975. Decisions of the courts based on this legislation have further elaborated the concept of family claims to inheritance.

Concern about the abuse of testamentary freedom and the growing view that this was a threat to the family led to a ten-year campaign for legislation which culminated in the enactment of the Inheritance (Family Provision) Act 1938 (Dainow, 1940: 337). Individual hard cases were publicised but there was no evidence of the extent of the problem. Rather the case for legislation was based on the fact that

England and Wales were out of step with Scotland, most of Europe, North America, and the Dominions in allowing such freedom of testamentary disposition. Proposals for a system of fixed shares for spouses and children, developed from the intestacy rules, were rejected and the 1938 Act was modelled on a New Zealand statute which gave the court discretion to make awards of reasonable provision where the will did not. Only a small minority of cases were expected to reach court (in New Zealand applications had only been made against 1.75 per cent of proved wills (Robson, 1938: 304)). Instead Lord Maugham, the Lord Chancellor, explained that the 1938 Act would change testamentary behaviour (Hansard, Lords Vol. 109 col. 802–3).

The attack on the principle of testamentary freedom was limited. Applications could only be made for maintenance by a surviving spouse, unmarried or disabled daughters, and sons who were either minors or disabled, where the will failed to make reasonable financial provision for them. If the surviving spouse was left not less than two-thirds of the income of the net estate, only children of a former marriage could apply. This prevented unseemly intra-family squabbles and indicated that a spouse had no claim to a greater share. The size of court orders was also limited to not more than two-thirds of the income where there were claims by a spouse and children, and to half of the income in other cases. Where the estate was worth less than £2,000 capital payments could be made to avoid the expense of administering a trust for claimants. These restrictions precluded the courts making orders in half the cases before them (Morton Report, 1951: 18) and discouraged claims against small estates. The courts were constantly cautious in their approach (Crane, 1957: 249). They interpreted their new powers conservatively, amending wills only where the provision (or its omission) was unreasonable. The scope of the 1938 Act was extended to intestacies by the Intestates' Estates Act 1952 which also allowed payments to take up the whole of the income and capital payments in estates of under £5,000. Further amendments allowed orders in favour of ex-spouses, removed all the financial limits on applications and orders, and gave a limited jurisdiction to the county court (Tyler, 1971: 8).

The restricted scope of this legislation, and the caution of the courts in interpreting it, meant that its impact on policy towards inheritance generally was bound to have been limited. Certainly it would be wrong to see the 1938 Act as having created a model for 'a reasonable will'.

Nonetheless it did reintroduce into English law, in a form suited to twentieth-century conditions, the idea that a widow or widower has claims on the spouse's estate. This is not surprising since much of the impetus for the 1938 Act came from the change in the rules of intestacy, introduced by the Administration of Estates Act 1925. (We discuss intestacy further in the following section.) Together these two pieces of legislation have served to emphasise that inheritance is not only about passing property down the generations. It is also—importantly—now about marriage and the financial responsibilities of spouses for each other. This theme was also prominent when the question came to public attention again in the 1970s.

In the early 1970s the Law Commission considered family provision during their Second Programme of Law Reform. Again the advantages of a discretion over a system of fixed rights (as applies in civil law jurisdictions) were considered and this time public opinion was sought. The majority of those questioned favoured automatic fixed rights (Todd and Jones, 1972: 47) which would have further limited testamentary freedom. However, the Law Commission concluded that such changes were neither necessary nor desirable, partly because of other proposals for co-ownership of the matrimonial home which would have protected the surviving spouse (Law Commission, 1973: 15). This occurred because, by the 1970s, public debate was influenced by the easier availability of divorce. Consideration about legislation on inheritance was bound to be influenced by the knowledge that, in the future, there would be many more cases where a testator was survived by more than one spouse or ex-spouse all of whom might feel that they had a moral claim on the estate. More generally, changes in the law on divorce and matrimonial property had served to strengthen the legal position of spouses. For example, the Matrimonial Proceedings and Property Act 1970 gave the courts wide powers to order the transfer of property on divorce, whereas previously they could only vary settlements (Denning, 1980: parts 7 and 8).

Hence, in considering changes in legislation on family provision the Law Commission's main concerns were the limitations of family provision law, particularly in comparison with the new broad powers to reallocate property following divorce. Maintenance alone could no longer be seen as the proper basis for determining provision for a surviving spouse (Law Commission, 1974: 5). Turning to other family members, the class of potential claimants was felt to be too narrow. The distinctions between sons and daughters could not be justified, and age limits did not adequately distinguish deserving cases. Dependants could claim loss of support under other legislation and in other jurisdictions: therefore family provision should be extended to them, it was argued (ibid: 22).

This represented a further challenge to testamentary freedom which was not uncontroversial, but these proposals were swiftly enacted as the Inheritance (Provision for Family and Dependants) Act 1975. The class of applicants was extended to include all children, step-children and any person dependent on the deceased, and the basis of awards for spouses was changed to bring it more into line with legislation on divorce. These changes had their impact on legal processes, making it more difficult for solicitors to advise testators whether their proposed dispositions might be overturned (Pettitt, 1978: 15). Although the test for overturning dispositions remained objective, namely that provision for the applicant was not reasonable, the courts were faced with a much wider range of circumstances to consider.

In reality it appears that only a small number of applications under the 1975 Act is made each year. According to the *Judicial Statistics*[2], in 1980 there were 651 applications, one for every 400 formally administered estates. However, this does not include an unknown number of applications made to the Family Division of the High Court which have never been shown in the published statistics. Moreover, figures for the county courts which before 1991 could only hear cases relating to estates under £30,000 (High Courts and County Courts Jurisdiction Order 1991 S.I. 1991 No. 724) are no longer published but applications to the Chancery Division of the High Court have declined since 1980 to under 200 a year. However, Legal Aid Statistics for 1993–4 (*Legal Aid*, 1994, 68) reveal that 1300 people were legally aided in proceedings under the Inheritance Act in that year. Legal Aid may be provided to more than one person in any proceedings so this does not indicate the number of wills challenged but it does suggest that Inheritance Act proceedings may be more common than the *Judicial Statistics* suggest. Nevertheless the number of applications is small compared with the number of estates administered which may reflect the fact that those dying in the late 1980s made their wills after the 1975 Act took effect and took account of its provisions in doing so.

[2] We have considered the evidence available in *Judicial Statistics* for the four sample years represented in our wills study. The full references for each year are: Cmnd.1126, 1959: Table 11, Cmnd.4419, 1969/70: Table 10, Cmnd.7977, 1979/80: Table D2(a), and Cmnd. 1154, 1989: Table 5.18.

Although 'negotiated' arrangements are made, there will normally be an application to protect the claimant and the solicitor if agreement is not reached, so a large number of hidden claims is unlikely.

In interpreting the law on family provisions, how much have the courts sought to clarify the underlying principles concerning the rights of different family members to make claims on the deceased's estate? Broadly the answer is that there is no consistent emphasis in any particular direction beyond acknowledging that the dependent spouse should normally be provided for. In fact reported cases reflect uncertainty amongst claimants, their advisers, and the judiciary. Taking these cases as a whole, the appropriate balance between a spouse and children is unclear although a life interest of a 'not insubstantial estate' for a widow was not held unreasonable in the case of *Davis* v *Davis* (1991) ([1993] 1 FLR 54). Some judges effectively rewrote wills to ensure equality in gifts to siblings (*Re Christie* [1979] Ch 168; *CA* v *CC* [1978] *The Times*, 17 November, 1978) whilst others discouraged applications by healthy adult sons (*Re Coventry* [1980] Ch 461; *Re Dennis* [1981] 2 All ER 140).

A further complication, with which the courts have had to deal, arises from the 1975 Act's requirement that a dependent claimant should not have given valuable consideration for the deceased's support. This has introduced a possible conflict of moral principles, in that it has made awards for the deserving problematic (Naresh, 1980: 534). It raises the possibility that someone who had cared for the deceased in his or her last illness, for example, might thereby be prevented from making a claim. This arises because the 1975 Act is not about rewarding kindness but supporting lost dependency. The solution suggested in the Court of Appeal was to take a common-sense approach, avoiding finely balanced computations but valuing the mutual love and support provided (*Bishop* v *Plumley* [1991] 1 WLR 582).

The influence of the Inheritance Acts should be determined from their effect on will-making behaviour generally rather than the number of applications before the courts. For example, books on will-making routinely refer to the powers under the Act. Nevertheless the vagueness of the statutory provisions, and the widely differing outcomes in reported cases, make it difficult to establish what impact the law has. More indirectly, we can argue that this legislation can be seen both as a reflection of contemporary ideas about the claims of different parties, and as a framework within which individuals will make bequeathing decisions, if they are aware of the law on this issue. We have already noted that the rights of spouses have been strengthened considerably. As far as children's rights are concerned, English law now recognises the claims of children where they have not been financially dependent upon the deceased parent. There is also some sense of what a child might reasonably expect a parent to have provided, given a particular station in life. For example, the 1975 Act provides for a child to claim support for the type of education which s/he might have expected, had the parent lived. However, even with family provision legislation in place, children's rights remain weak relative to those in civil law jurisdictions.

Perpetuities

We have spent some time on the Inheritance Acts because they represent the main way, for the majority of the population, in which the law has introduced restrictions on testamentary freedom in the twentieth century. However, there are two other kinds of restriction, both of which developed earlier. These are the rule against perpetuities, developed in the seventeenth century, and the doctrine of mutual wills established in the eighteenth century. We consider each of them in turn.

The rule against perpetuities developed to cope with a practical problem which also raises some fundamental questions about testamentary freedom. At the heart of a property system which allows complete testamentary freedom is the basic paradox that uncontrolled freedom can be self-destructive (Moffat and Chesterman, 1988: 259). This becomes obvious if one imagines a situation where the law allows a will in which the testator determines to whom the property shall pass, not merely on his or her own death, but also in succeeding generations. This is precisely what land-owning families tried to do during the fifteenth, sixteenth, and seventeenth centuries, in an attempt to lock property into the direct succession from father to eldest son (the common law in fact had already permitted this to be done but only for two descendent generations). The effect of such arrangements is to remove the freedom of testamentary disposition from succeeding generations, giving them only a life interest in the property (Simpson, 1986). Therefore the donor's freedom to control the destination and use of donated property can deny the recipient the freedom to enjoy it fully. The rule against perpetuities which developed in the seventeenth century sought to balance the interests of competing generations by limiting the power to establish dynastic trusts. It permitted a settlor to give life estates to his wife and children and provide for unborn grandchildren during their minority (Simes, 1954: 729) but a gift which might vest outside that period was void.

The rule against perpetuities lost much of its significance with provisions facilitating the sale of trust property. Taxation became a strong influence; any action which precluded flexible response to it was likely to undermine rather than protect wealth. However, the need for the rule was never seriously questioned in principle, even when reform was being considered in the 1950s. Modifications reducing its harsher impacts were introduced in 1964, but the rule against perpetuities remains in place. Much more recently, the issue has come back into focus with the need for legal control of dynasticism now being questioned. The rule was abolished in Manitoba in 1983 and is under consideration by the Law Commission in England (Law Commission, 1993b).

The complexity of the rule against perpetuities means that it is fully understood by few practising lawyers and that it is unlikely to play a major part when advice is given about writing wills. To anticipate our discussion in later chapters, the rather small number of gifts in wills to grandchildren in our own study does not suggest a strong desire to give property directly to subsequent generations, although the tax advantages may encourage the wealthy to make such gifts (Inland Revenue, 1988: 3.8).

Mutual wills

In contrast with the Inheritance Acts and the rule against perpetuities, the restriction on testamentary freedom resulting from the doctrine of mutual wills is self-imposed. Mutual wills entail an agreement by two testators to leave property in a particular way, usually to each other and then to beneficiaries chosen jointly. Though the survivor can revoke the will, the terms of the original agreement will be enforced. Thus the law provides the means to enforce 'joint' choices, and to that extent its support for mutual wills is a restriction on the freedom of testamentary disposition for the individual who survives. Alternatively, it can be argued that both individuals have chosen to deny themselves ultimate testamentary freedom.

The extent of this self-denial is unknown. Married couples are encouraged to make wills together and solicitors generally charge lower fees for this, but mutual wills could only exist where the spouses have agreed to this. Each person has to weigh up the potential advantage to his or her beneficiaries against the loss of the freedom to change their will. If neither expects their circumstances to change nor intends to review their will regularly, both may be willing to accept the obligation. It must also be acknowledged that in many cases individual wills may be made which have the same effect, in practice, as mutual wills but without the force of law, resulting simply from family members reinforcing each other's views about the proper dispositions. Wills themselves of course cannot reveal the extent of such informal agreements.

In summary, we would argue that in England and Wales legal restrictions on testamentary freedom remain marginal and are unlikely to play a prominent part when people write their wills. Such a view does not deny the influence of law on will-making but suggests a more complex interaction including other legal and non-legal influences on behaviour.

The significance of wills for the transmission of property

Because this book is specifically about wills, so far in this discussion of the law we have concentrated on legal aspects of will-making. But it is important to place this in a broader context. In what ways does the law support and facilitate the transmission of property outside a will, either after the death or during the lifetime of a donor?

We begin with an issue where English law is reluctant to intervene, namely situations where someone claims that the deceased had promised to bequeath some property to him or her but has not put this into effect through provisions in a will. English law will not usually enforce such a promise unless it can be construed as a contract and, within the family context in particular, there is a reluctance to accept that the parties intend to create a legally enforceable agreement. Also English contract law requires the promisee to give consideration. If the testator's promise is gratuitous or the would-be beneficiary is being rewarded for past kindnesses, it is not possible to construe the arrangements as a contract or to enforce it.

Although the courts have used the principles of proprietary estoppel or constructive trusts to provide a remedy to a disappointed beneficiary (*Re Basham* [1987] 1 All ER 405) this does not amount to any general recognition that such promises should be enforced. On the contrary, their enforcement may be seen as conflicting with the principles set out in the Wills Act 1837. By contrast, other common law jurisdictions which allow broad testamentary freedom have developed remedies which allow the promisee to claim against the deceased's estate. In New Zealand, the Law Reform (Testamentary Promises) Act 1949 enables a person who was promised a testamentary gift for or as a result of services provided to claim the value of the services or even the specific item promised. In Canada, the courts have allowed claims based on the principle of *quantum meruit* (Davey, 1988).

However, it would be wrong to conclude from this example of promises that under English law property passes only through the formal mechanism of a will. In reality, wills determine the transmission of only a proportion of property transferred on death. In part this is because will-making remains a minority activity; less than a third of the deceased leave a will which is admitted to probate.[3] The other two-thirds either do not make a will or leave a will which is not probated. Wills only become public documents (and therefore available for research) when probate is granted, but where the estate consists of relatively small amounts in, for example, insurance policies or savings accounts, probate is not necessary (Administration of Estates (Small Payments) Act 1965). The will should still determine the distribution of assets, although surviving relatives sometimes make very different arrangements (Abel-Smith, Zander, and Brooke, 1973: 130). The number of unprobated last wills is unknown but if a survey of will-making intention is a true reflection of what people actually do—which of course is unlikely—twice as many wills may be made as are probated (Law Commission, 1989: 25). None of this implies that wills are unimportant in the transmission of property. We need to make a distinction between the number of *people* who make wills and the amount of *property* which passes by this means. In fact substantial amounts of property are distributed via wills. Those who die testate are generally thought to leave more property than those without wills (Miller, 1977: 89) though published data do not straightforwardly support this conclusion, as we shall indicate in the next chapter (see

[3] This widely quoted statistic is an estimate which can be obtained by the following calculation: a comparison made between the number of probated wills for a given year (obtained from the *Judicial Statistics* referred to in note 2 to this chapter) and the Registrar General's statistics on deaths of adults for the same year. The relevant tables are to be found respectively in the: Registrar General's Statistical Review for 1959 (Table 14), 1969 (Table 14), 1979 (Table 10), and 1989 (Table 3) (all HMSO). Such a comparison must necessarily produce an estimate rather than an accurate figure since a will may not be probated in the same calendar year in which the death of the testator occurred.

especially Figure 3.3). Moreover, wills have also influenced the rules of intestacy; the pattern of disposition under intestacy legislation was formulated and reformed by reference to gift patterns in wills (ibid: 17).

Turning to the issue of intestacy, this can be seen as a means by which the state provides a 'statutory will' (Russell Committee, 1966: para. 3) for the intestate presuming his or her intentions to be like those of testators. The devolution of an intestate's estate depends on which relations survive and the size of the estate (see Figure. 2.1). The rules, introduced in 1926, combine two ideas: protection for the deceased's dependants and entitlement to inheritance amongst genealogically closer relatives. Intestacy rules therefore are of some importance in identifying the law's understanding of families, and of the respective claims of different family members, in matters related to inheritance.

Under intestacy the surviving spouse is protected by provision of a statutory legacy. From December 1993 the amount is £200,000 if there are no children and £125,000 if there are surviving children (Family Provision (Intestate Succession) Order 1993 (SI 1993 No. 2906). This exhausts the estate in the majority of cases; in the case of larger estates, spouses also receive a life interest (or absolute interest if there are no children) in half the residue. Dependent children are generally protected by providing resources to the surviving spouse who is usually their parent, but where the estate is substantial children receive a share directly. The deceased's parents and siblings inherit if there are no children, but after a larger sum has been allocated to the surviving spouse. More distant relatives, grandparents, uncles, and aunts inherit only where there are no closer relatives. Cousins were excluded from the list of beneficiaries because of the cost of tracing them (Hansard, Commons, Vol. 155, col. 455, 1922).

Intestacy rules therefore focus mainly on the blood line, favouring genealogically close relatives before more distant ones, and descendent generations before ascendant. Alongside this is the principle that dependants should be provided for. Though this applies both to children and to spouses, the latter are numerically much more important since now very few people die before their children reach adulthood and most adult children would not be financially dependent on their parents. As with Family Provision legislation therefore, the strengthening of the intestacy rules has tended to make spouses more central to legal processes related to inheritance. Recently, a case was made that the scales should be tipped even further. In 1989 the Law

FIG. 2.1. Devolution of property on intestacy

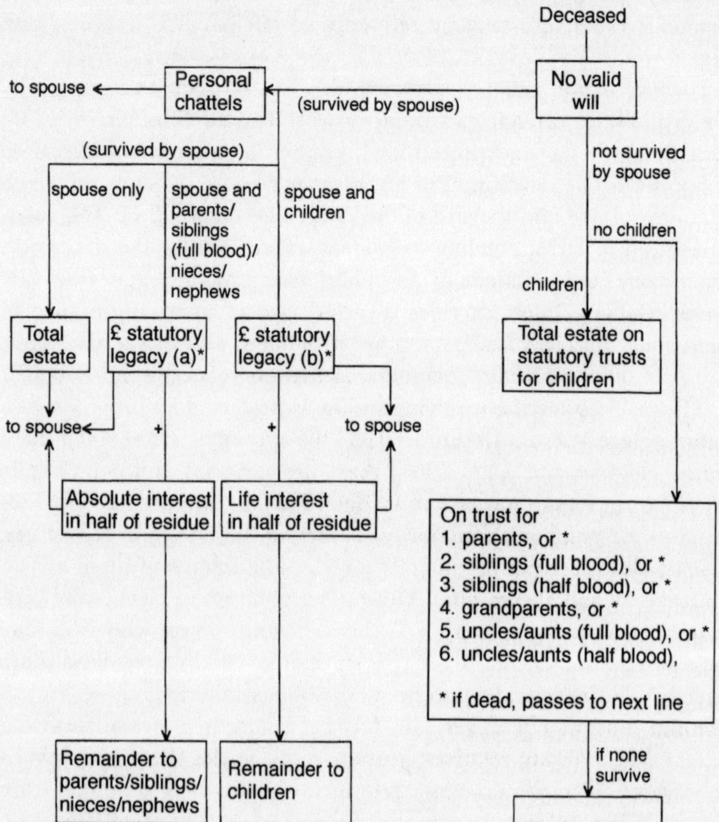

*Spouse's statutory legacy

	(a) no children	(b) with children
1959	£20,000	£5,000
1969	£30,000	£8,750
1979	£55,000	£25,000
1989	£125,000	£75,000
1993	£200,000	£125,000

Commission proposed that the surviving spouse should receive the whole of the estate (Law Commission, 1989: 9) but this realignment of the balance between spouse and family has been widely criticised (Miller, 1993: 182; Cretney, 1995: 77) and not included in the Law Reform (Succession) Bill.

Another way in which property is transmitted outside wills is through gifts made during the lifetime of the donor. Substantial amounts of property pass by *inter vivos* gift, perhaps reflecting the donor's desire to enjoy the recipient's reward and also to obtain the tax advantages of this form of giving. *Inter vivos* gifts were estimated to be worth 10 per cent of the net capital value of all estates assessed for duty in 1968 and to be increasing (Horsman, 1975: 521–2). (We return to this issue of *inter vivos* gifts, in the context of our own study, in chapter 3).

Trusts established either *inter vivos* or by will can be used to control the transfer of property over a number of generations. In the past family trust settlements were an important method in wealthy families of transferring property between generations and controlling its use, but changes in the tax system and the need to be able to respond to future changes have made such devices far less attractive during this century (Crane, 1957: 242). However, the option remains in place, and certainly can be attractive for tax purposes to families with substantial wealth. So, even though a substantial proportion of personal wealth remains tied up in this way, the number of discretionary trusts is thought to be declining (Inland Revenue, 1980: 45; idem, 1988: 3.7) and such considerations are irrelevant to the majority of people. This is important because much scholarly discussion of inheritance focuses on tax questions. This may serve to obscure the real meaning which inheritance has for the majority of the population.

Of more general relevance are other ways in which valuable assets pass on death without a will. Most occupational pension schemes provide for a widow's and a widower's pension on the death of the scheme member. The state also provides widow's pensions. These valuable assets accrue because of the recipient's status, not the wishes of the spouse. Many occupational schemes also provide substantial lump sums up to four times the member's salary which can be nominated in favour of any beneficiary if the member dies before retirement. Such property passes outside the will and is not subject to inheritance tax. The value of occupational pension rights and the coverage of schemes has grown markedly in the last thirty years. Approximately 50 per cent of employed people are scheme members. In 1987 pension scheme holdings amounted to nearly 20 per cent of all personal wealth, and pensions in payment amounted to more than twice the amount of property which passed through estates (Government Actuary, 1991: tables 2.1 and 4.9).

Small amounts (up to £5,000 under current legislation) held in a savings account or payable as a result of life assurance may be transferred by the less formal process of nomination (Administration of Estates (Small Payments) Act 1965) which is sometimes referred to as a 'poor man's will'. The insured usually only needs to complete a form naming the intended beneficiary and send it to the insurance company. Next of kin can close accounts if they show the death certificate.

Another important point affecting large numbers of people is that, where property is held jointly, it passes automatically by survivorship to the surviving joint owners and not via the will (Cretney and Masson, 1990: 245). Joint ownership is most likely between married couples for assets such as a joint bank account or the matrimonial car or home. This practice is now widespread; for example, a study of maintenance after divorce found that 81 per cent of childless couples and 72 per cent of couples with children held property in joint names (Eekelaar and Maclean, 1986). A different study of financial arrangements between married couples found that over half had a joint bank account or common kitty, out of which common expenses were paid (Pahl, 1989: 71). Joint ownership may thus exclude valuable assets from the formal processes of inheritance. It is unclear how people decide between ownership of houses as 'joint tenancies', to which survivorship applies, and the other form of co-ownership ('tenancies in common'), or indeed the extent to which owners understand the distinction. Emphasis on the individual's own share, flexibility, and tax-planning support 'tenancies in common', but the notion of marriage as a partnership of equals and the widespread practice of leaving most property to the spouse suggest the use of 'joint tenancies'. Trends over time are equally hard to discern. There seems to have been a move to co-ownership of the matrimonial home away from sole ownership by the husband, but the form of co-ownership remains uncertain.

Where the deceased rents property, there is usually no interest to pass on by will, but the law provides for the transmission of residential tenancies to a member of the tenant's family living with him or her at the date of death. Recent changes have limited most of these rights to allow only a single transfer, rather than two. Again it is the status and the residence of the recipient which determine what happens to the property rather than the deceased's will. Similar provisions apply to some rented agricultural property.

Thus, taking the total picture of the transmission of property, it is clear that wills play a relatively small role in quantitative terms, though one which is significant in establishing underlying principles. Where a deceased person is survived by a spouse, it is likely that the more important route for the transmission of assets is some combination of: property which passes automatically because it is jointly owned; assets such as pension rights which pass outside the will; and the operation of the intestacy rules. For the majority of people, decisions about the transmission of property which enable the exercise of testamentary freedom really become relevant only if they have outlived their own spouse. At this point, in reality, decisions about how to divide an estate become much more open.

Concluding remarks

The purpose of this chapter has been to outline the legal context against which the content of English wills needs to be judged. In so doing, we have been able to make a number of points which we will carry forward in subsequent chapters.

First, we can return to the research questions which we posed at the end of chapter 1 concerning the content of wills, in particular what they reveal about people's concepts of 'family' and the relative claims of different family members. It can now be seen that these questions have a particular resonance in the context of the English legal system. The fact that English law gives priority to the principle of testamentary freedom means that questions about how people choose to dispose of their property are more interesting and more important than they would be under jurisdictions where testators are required to leave set proportions of their estate to relatives identified in law. We can also see that the opportunities to exercise it in practice are much greater for someone who has outlived her or his spouse, or has not been married, than for people who make their last will in the context of a 'live' marriage.

Second, and despite a continuing emphasis on testamentary freedom, we can see that the law does acknowledge the claims of different family members in certain circumstances through legislation on family provision, where the courts have to interpret ambiguous wills and when someone has died intestate. The claims acknowledged reveal a mixture of principles in various combinations: that economic dependants should continue to be supported from the deceased's estate; that genealogical closeness in the blood line should govern the strength of claims; and, increasingly, that a surviving spouse's claim should take precedence over others. In analysing our own sample of wills, we will make comparisons with these principles implicit in the law.

Third, we need to acknowledge that wills tell only part of the story of how property gets transmitted from one individual, and from one generation, to the next. Certain valuable assets pass outside wills, and of course a significant proportion of the population dies intestate. However, even here, the decisions of people who do make wills are important, in that these influence the shape of the intestacy rules.

3 Making a Will

In this chapter we focus on will-making as a process. We also begin to draw on data from our own sample of 800 wills, comparing them with other studies where relevant. First, we discuss the legal regulation of will-making, not in terms of the content of the will (which we covered in chapter 2) but in terms of the form which a will must take and the process through which it must be drawn up. Second, we consider how far will-making can be considered as a 'planning' process from the testator's perspective. Third, we discuss the social and economic context of will-making, posing the questions: who makes a will, and under what life circumstances are wills made? Finally, we complete our overview of will-making as a process by discussing how estates are administered after a death, and we outline some evidence about testators' wishes concerning this part of the process.

A valid will

In general, a will is only valid if it is made by an adult who has the mental capacity to determine the destination of his or her property and who complies with the formal requirements of the Wills Act 1837. Briefly wills, and any changes to them, must be in writing, signed by the testator and witnessed by two people. The content of the will is a matter for the testator but it should appoint an executor and dispose of all the testator's property. The testator's mode of expression is important because rules of construction have developed to aid interpretation; for example, before 1970 a gift to 'children' would normally have benefited only legitimate children.

Legal commentators see these formalities as serving four distinct functions: to provide evidence of the testator's intentions, to warn the testator to think seriously, to protect the testator from undue influence, and to make the process of transmitting large amounts of property smooth and efficient (Langbein, 1975: 494). Where these requirements are satisfied the will 'speaks from death' passing all the remaining property as the testator intended, but it remains revocable, leaving the testator's freedom to deal with the property during life intact.

If we look at this from the perspective developed in previous chapters, namely that wills are at the same time both public and private documents, we can see that the tight regulation of the process of will-making is a corollary to the relative lack of regulation of the contents of a will. What do these type of regulations about the form which a will must take, and the process whereby wills are to be made, tell us about the balance between private wishes and public interest? Essentially they demonstrate that, in a jurisdiction which allows considerable testamentary freedom concerning the *contents* of a will, there is in fact a public interest in ensuring that the *form* and *process* of will-making is tightly regulated to ensure that property is transmitted in a manner which is clear and orderly. The state takes a close interest in whether a particular document is to count as a will, and in ensuring that any ambiguity about its terms is minimised or eliminated. This is not surprising since so much hangs upon the provisions of each will. The state also has an interest in ensuring that testators are capable of making decisions which are reason*ed* (even though those decisions may not seem reason*able* to other people), hence the provisions about 'testamentary capacity' built into the legislation. Though in practice these are quite tricky to handle (Law Reform Committee, 1980: para. 2.18), the principle remains that a will can only be valid if the testator can be assumed to have had the mental capacity to make a will at the time it was drawn up. Again it is clear that the public interest requires close attention to be paid to the circumstances under which each will is made, since so much depends on it.

The clearest symbolic expression of the public interest in the process of will-making is the provision that the will must be signed in the presence of two witnesses, who must also attest and sign. This makes the process a semi-public one, even though the will itself is not immediately publicly available. Commentators tend to underscore the point about the public interest by emphasising the 'ritual' elements introduced into the signing of a will by these provisions. Making it into this type of semi-public ritual in a sense ensures that the testator sees it as a significant event which s/he must take seriously, and which therefore should not be conducted too casually, it is argued (Law Reform Committee, 1980: para. 2.10; Mellows, 1983: 56–7).

There is no requirement to seek professional advice when making a will although the majority of testators do so. Of the wills in our study, 81.5 per cent appeared to have been drafted professionally, and comparable figures have been observed in other surveys (Justice,

1971: 1; Law Reform Committee, 1980: 31). In our sample men and women were equally likely to use professional assistance when making their will. Evidence from elsewhere suggests that home-made wills are slightly more likely to fail to comply with the strict rules about making a will although this appears to occur rarely: only 0.24 per cent of a 1979 sample were rejected (Law Reform Committee, 1980: 31). However, some more obviously defective 'wills' may be rejected without ever being submitted to probate. Home-made wills may be a problem for the legal profession (Pettitt, 1978: 3) and may fail to reflect the testator's true intentions (Justice, 1971: 3), but reform either by imposing restrictions or removing formalities is thought unnecessary or undesirable (Miller, 1977: 152).

In relation to the actual format in which wills are written, there is much less variation in practice than in principle the law would allow, especially where solicitors have been involved in drafting. Although professionally made wills are drafted individually, in the sense that the will is produced only after an interview with the client during which his or her intentions are determined, it is generally drafted using existing precedents. Precedents—specimen clauses which are designed to produce specific outcomes—are widely used by the legal profession. There are many published versions, including a comprehensive Encyclopaedia of Forms and Precedents. Further, practitioners' texts on wills generally include precedents for all common forms of gift. Individual solicitors also devise precedents using their own preferred form of wording and these may be used by colleagues within a firm to produce a 'house style', a practice no doubt facilitated by the widespread availability of word processors. Published precedents for wills traditionally are listed under the types of testator for whom each would be deemed most relevant, for example 'Wills of spinsters and bachelors' and 'Wills of married persons'. This may also extend to occupational categories, for example 'Wills of farmers' or 'Wills of traders'.

Thus precedents are at the same time both individual and impersonal. They are individual in that they are selected or written by the person drawing up the will to satisfy the wishes of the particular testator. But they are also general or impersonal, in that the same formulation is used for many testators. Inevitably therefore precedents act as a form of standardization in the drafting of wills.

The two examples given below are taken from a 1964 book of precedents (George and George, 1964), reflecting the thinking from a period during which many of the wills in our study were written. We have selected two contrasting formulae because they enable us to illustrate two different types of will, whose significance has been revealed through our own analysis, as we shall show in later chapters. The first is an example of what we are calling a 'total estate will', in which all the testator's property is bequeathed as a single entity ('the estate'). In the example given, the estate is bequeathed intact to a single individual; in other cases, it may be divided proportionately between several beneficiaries. The second example is of the type we have labelled a 'composite will' because the estate is divided into specific gifts and a gift of the residue. The latter example also shows the gendered assumptions behind specific bequests, which are discussed in later chapters on patterns of giving.

EXAMPLE 1. Will giving the whole of a testator's property to a named beneficiary.

I (testator) of . . . HEREBY REVOKE all wills and testamentary dispositions heretofore made by me and DECLARE this to be my last will I DEVISE AND BEQUEATH all the real and personal property whatsoever and wheresoever to which I may be entitled or over which I have any disposing power at the time of my death unto A of . . . absolutely and I APPOINT the said A to be the sole executor of this my will.

EXAMPLE 2. Will of a bachelor giving the residue of his estate to his nephews and nieces at twenty-five.

(*Note*: the precedent for this situation begins by referring to the standard precedents for establishing the testator's identity, revoking previous wills, and appointing executors and trustees. It then continues as follows.)

Specific bequests

2. I give the following bequests to the following persons:
   (a) To Alfred Morgan my clothes wearing apparel books and gold watch.
   (b) etc.

Pecuniary legacies

3. I give the following legacies to the following persons:
   (a) To Beatrice Hale the sum of . . .
   (b) To Caroline Thomas contingently on her attaining the age of twenty-five years the sum of . . . which said sum shall be set apart by my Trustees and accumulated by investing the same and the income produced thereby so as to form one fund.
   (c) To the Missions for Seamen the sum of . . . and I DECLARE that the

receipt of the person purporting to be the Secretary or Treasurer thereof for the time being shall be an absolute discharge to my Trustees.

Gift of residue

4. I GIVE the residue of my estate wheresoever and whatsoever to my Trustees UPON TRUST to pay my debts and funeral and testamentary expenses and estate duty payable on my death and subject thereto to divide the same between such of my nephews and nieces as shall attain the age of twenty-five years but so nevertheless that John Rowland shall take a double share and if only one shall attain the age of twenty-five years then for him or her absolutely PROVIDED that (i) if any of my nephews or nieces shall die in my lifetime or shall survive me but fail to attain the age of twenty-five years and in either case shall leave child or children who shall attain the age of twenty-one years or marry then such child or children shall take and if more than one in equal shares the share which his or her or their parent would have taken had he survived me and attained the age of twenty-five years (ii) if any of my nephews or nieces shall not have attained the age of four years at the date of my death then the age of twenty-one years shall be substituted for the age of twenty-five years in this clause so far as relates to such nephew or niece.

Our own sample of 800 wills certainly confirms that the use of precedents of this type is widespread, occurring routinely in professionally written wills and also being reflected in many home-made wills where testators were using a standardized will-making form. The use of precedents certainly standardizes the format of wills in practice, even though this is not a requirement of the law, and to some extent it may also be seen as standardizing their content.

Will-making as a planning process

Although adults can make a will at any time by jotting their disposition on the back of an envelope, it was clear from our sample of wills that will-making was almost always a planned activity. Our sample contains no cases of used envelopes though there are one or two example of wills apparently written on note paper, which could denote a decision to make a will on the spur of the moment. However, in the vast majority of cases, our testators had taken the trouble to consult a professional or, at least, to purchase a form on which to write their will. These forms are readily available from stationers, but their use indicates that the will was not made without prior thought. Before taking these steps, the intending testators must recognise their need to make a will and be sufficiently concerned about their property to want to make arrangements for its disposition. Unless the destination of property matters, there is little point in making a will. So the evidence of our data is that will-making is an activity which people plan in advance of doing it, at least to some extent.

In principle it is possible that *not* making a will equally constitutes a 'planned' act. It is possible for a person to decide that the intestacy rules provide for exactly what they wish to do. Indeed development of these rules from common patterns in wills might be expected to make this the case. However, intestacy can only be a rational choice by someone who is fully cognisant of the rules. Three-quarters of those questioned for the Law Commission Study had some knowledge of what would happen to their estate if they were to die intestate, and half had had some experience in intestacy (Law Commission, 1989: 26); an earlier study suggested that only 10 per cent had accurate knowledge (Todd and Jones, 1972: 36–7) . Solicitors, if consulted, are unlikely to advise any but those with the most limited assets that intestacy rules provide adequately. Changes in the size of the estate, the family composition or even the law could mean that the distribution on intestacy or the incidence of taxation was quite different from that intended, with the possibility of liability on the adviser to disappointed beneficiaries. Moreover, the amount of time required to clarify these issues with a client is only slightly greater if a will is drafted, yet it may be easier to make a more economic charge than where only advice is provided. Drafting a will is more likely to lead to profitable business in winding up the estate than if the solicitor had merely provided advice, for whose source relatives would have no tangible evidence.

Thus the professional pressures are all in the direction of encouraging people to make wills. Increasingly, potential will-makers are also exposed to more public forms of pressure. Campaigns such as the Law Society's 'Make a Will Week', charity literature, and guides on will-making use a variety of approaches to overcome potential resistance. Making a will is linked by slogans such as 'Fight Cancer with a Will' (Imperial Cancer Research Fund) and 'Make a will, make a difference' (Christian Aid) linking charitable giving with self-interest. The Law Society's campaign reinforced this by providing a will without charge in return for a donation to charity, at the same time seeking to dispel the idea that using a solicitor is an expensive business. In contrast, intestacy is portrayed as irresponsible and immoral: 'more men are guilty of intestacy than adultery' (World Wildlife Fund). Fear of will-making is countered with dire and exaggerated warnings about the consequences of intestacy: for example, the family home may need to be sold to pay tax or your property may be forfeited to the Crown (*Which?*, 1991: 9).

Precisely what influences people to take this step of making a will is rather elusive, though later in this chapter we consider data from our own study, which give some clues to this. In this section we concentrate on asking: when someone has decided to take the step of making a will, what kinds of 'planning' are involved? Even though the act of writing a will may be 'planned', this tells us little about the kinds of *forward* planning in which testators may engage. So the answer to this question is not straightforward since testators' opportunities to plan the disposal of their property are limited by lack of knowledge of the eventual circumstances surrounding their death, particularly the size of their assets, the extent of their social network, and the position of their potential beneficiaries. The majority of testators are exposed to professional advisers who may raise their awareness of their obligations, of the incentives provided in tax law and of possible alternative ways of satisfying their intentions. Indeed advisers may even determine the contents of the will (Pettitt, 1978: 6). In a small study of professional advisers which we have also undertaken, some solicitors interviewed stated that this was the inevitable consequence of advising someone who was uncertain of their own intentions (Masson, 1994; Finch, Mason, Hayes, and Wallis, forthcoming).

The evidence of our wills study suggests that professionals have become more influential over the last forty years. The proportion of those making their wills independently has declined from 31 per cent in the 1959 sample to 11.5 per cent in 1989. If we use, as our measure of change over time, the date when the will was written as opposed to the date of death (see chapter 1 for discussion of this measure), then a clear pattern emerges. Twenty-nine per cent of wills written in the 1950s were home-made, but for wills written in the 1960s this dropped sharply to 13 per cent, remaining at around that level to the most recent examples in the 1980s, where the figure was 12 per cent (significant at the .00 level). There is also a marked and increasing difference between the values of the estates in professionally made and home-made wills. The median value of the estates of those who made their own wills was £1,089 in our 1959 sample and £3,940 in 1979, less than 50 per cent and less than 25 per cent respectively of the median values for professionally made wills for the same years. Thus it seems to be predominantly people with small estates who make home-made wills and increasingly so over time. It may be that those with fewer assets are more concerned about the cost of professional help, and have less experience of using professionals for other purposes (since, for example, the size of their estates makes it unlikely that many of them own a house). However, they may simply consider that there is no need to seek help because they have little property, although they are sufficiently concerned to make a formal will.

Thus the planning observed in wills is the combined effect of legal, professional, and social influences on testators, mediated, in most cases, through the words chosen by professionals to achieve the ends which testators have chosen after being advised. In the case of home-made wills, professional influence is more limited but cannot be presumed to be absent. Testators must have acquired some information to want to make a formal will and may have consulted books, asked acquaintances or read the guidance notes provided with standard will forms.

The idea of planning is encapsulated in the term 'estate planner' which is sometimes used for those who draft wills. Such a term flatters to deceive, using the term 'estate' in relation to modest assets and focusing on tax avoidance rather than the need to prepare for death generally (Shaffer, 1970: 1). From a legal perspective, there are three distinct elements to planning the distribution of property on death: planning and executing the testator's wishes, planning for dependants, and tax planning. Although the testator's prime concern is frequently the care of dependants (Shaffer, 1970: 80) and the size of the estate may mean that it must all be directed to this end, this is not always the case. Testamentary freedom is not absolute and advice on its limits is included in the standard works on will drafting.

The planning process involves establishing the current value and general composition of the available property, the composition of the testator's family, their needs, and what are the testator's current intentions. The client may be asked to consider these matters and even to provide a list of their main assets in preparation for the meeting with the adviser. Alternatively, details may be recorded on a pro-forma during an interview. Where the potential estate is large, further advice from an accountant may be recommended. The adviser needs to be clear what the testator intends, that the provision for dependants is reasonable (and thus unlikely to be challenged under the Inheritance Act 1975), and that all eventualities are covered.

Planning may be easiest when the will is made close to death so that the value of assets and the positions of intended beneficiaries are unlikely to change. Interviewees in our advisers' study commented that clients rarely thought that their children might predecease them or that the family would perish in a common catastrophe (Masson, 1994; Finch, Mason, Hayes, and Wallis, forthcoming). However, from the perspective of the legal profession clients have to contemplate these unthinkable events and make decisions to cover them. Provision is made for these hypothetical situations by providing progressions so that the will still operates to dispose of the property in an intended way although it was drafted primarily for very different circumstances. Chapter 6 discusses such progressions in our own wills sample. This device is used because it cannot be assumed that all testators regularly review and remake their wills, and it is always possible that someone who might wish to do so will lack the capacity when the need arises. In our own study it was impossible to determine how many testators had made a previous will. Many wills contained clauses revoking earlier wills but this does not constitute usable evidence, since solicitors' clients are advised to include it in all cases to prevent continued searching after a will is found (Bailey, 1967: 94). However, the significant proportion of wills in our sample made long before death (24.5 per cent made ten or more years before death) and the small number of codicils (59 out of 800) both suggest that regular updating of wills is uncommon.

We conclude therefore that, in most cases, a will is intended to last to the testator's death. Planning for a will with lasting qualities has further implications for the form which gifts should take. From a legal perspective, proportions of the estate are preferable to cash sums because of the changing value of money and the possibility that the estate on death will be worth less or more than when the will was drafted. For similar reasons, gifts of specific items and of sums in particular bank accounts, which would be ineffective if the property was disposed of, are likely to be discouraged by professional advisers. The planning process may also influence the allocation of proportionate shares because, for example, a current justification for inequality between beneficiaries such as need or deserts may not apply when the testator dies.

The question of tax planning is clearly the most technically complex aspect of will-making and it is unlikely to be a factor in the case of home-made wills. The importance of tax planning to the average testator has changed markedly over the last forty years with the amendment and abolition of Estate Duty, its replacement with Capital Transfer Tax, recast and renamed Inheritance Tax in 1986. The proportion of all formally administered estates which are large enough to be subject to tax has declined from 25 per cent in 1959 to 16 per cent in 1989, and the proportion where tax is levied has declined further to 9 per cent, largely because of the complete exemption, under Inheritance Tax, for gifts between spouses. The change in the significance of death duties is perhaps most clear from the decline in the proportion of tax revenue raised in this way from 7.5 per cent in 1969/70 to 1.6 per cent in 1989/90, as reflected in Inland Revenue statistics for the relevant years.

Nevertheless tax planning may influence both the use of wills and their drafting. An Inland Revenue study of discretionary trusts indicated differences in the beneficiaries, investments, and application of income between those established in life and on death (Inland Revenue, 1988: 3.6). For most of the period of our study *inter vivos* gifts have been subject to a preferential tax regime. Before 1968, this applied to gifts made more than five years before death; between 1969 and 1974, and after 1986, the period was seven years. Accurate figures for *inter vivos* gifts are not available but Horsman (1975: 521) estimated that £177 million in Estate Duty was saved in 1967/68 through lifetime gifts, approximately 10 per cent of the net capital value of all estates assessed for duty in that year. Such gifts are probably used to a greater extent today because other methods of avoiding tax, particularly the use of discretionary trusts, have become less effective (as we indicated in chapter 2).

In our sample of wills there is little direct evidence of tax planning having influenced the form of the will, though it is possible that it occurred in some cases without the wills giving any hint of this. It is also possible to misinterpret provisions in a will as an indication of tax planning. An example of this would be the use of life interest provisions before 1974. Under the Estate Duty regime there were advantages in settling property on a spouse to provide only a life interest; tax was only payable on the value of the life interest rather than the whole capital sum and on the spouse's death no further duty was levied in respect of the remainder. There was no need to limit a spouse's share under Capital Transfer Tax (or Inheritance Tax) because of the complete exemption for transfers between spouses. A greater use of life interests in wills drafted before 1974 could indicate tax planning. Equally, however, it could have been done for other reasons. The spectre of the unintended life interest is repeatedly raised in discussions about wills, especially those made without advice (Law Reform Committee,

1973: paras. 23, 60; Justice, 1971: 3), and the Inheritance (Family Provision) Act 1938 meant that such a gift was unlikely to be challenged. Meanwhile the non-use of life interests would not necessarily show lack of tax planning, given the high proportion of small estates where the life interest in favour of a wife would generally have been considered ill-advised because the income alone would not provide adequately for her needs (Pettitt, 1978: 14).

A similar point can be made about 'generation skipping', which avoids the incidence of taxation by ensuring that property is passed directly to beneficiaries in the second or third generation (children or grandchildren) rather than through someone in the testator's generation. There is some evidence of this (Diamond Commission, 1977: 176; Inland Revenue, 1988: 3.8) but the Inland Revenue concluded in 1980 that most property was being taxed every generation (Inland Revenue, 1980: 49). Tax planning is not the only reason for such gifts; need may encourage a grandparent to pass property to young adult grandchildren. But greater use by those with larger estates and thus potentially higher liability might indicate tax planning, although it is only the wealthier who could exercise such choice.

We conclude therefore that wills themselves yield little clear evidence of whether tax planning is taking place widely. However, we suspect that it is not, both on the basis of our advisers study (Masson, 1994) and on the basis of interviews with members of the general public about their own approach to inheritance questions (Finch, Mason, Hayes, and Wallis, forthcoming). Both offer evidence that few people see tax planning as relevant to their own circumstances, as indeed in many cases it is not, because the size of the estate is too modest. The other dimensions of 'planning' involved in a will would seem to figure more prominently with most people.

Finally, it should be noted that planning need not involve the deceased but may occur 'post-mortem'. Beneficiaries may disclaim so that the property passes on intestacy, or vary the will by redirecting gifts to a chosen person. If this action is taken within two years of the death, the gifts are treated as if they were made by the will (or intestacy). There can be major tax advantages of such action, for example making use of the nil-rate band, but non-tax factors such as provision for someone omitted from a will are usually more significant (Whitehouse and Stuart-Buttle, 1990: 385), though again the extent of such re-arrangement is unknown. Most of the solicitors interviewed in our advisers study had some experience of it, advising beneficiaries of the possibilities on occasion (Masson, 1994).

To summarise, we see will-making both as a 'planned' and as a 'planning' process. It is planned in the sense that testators undertake it typically as a conscious act, not on the spur of the moment. It entails planning in several senses. In considering the provisions of the will, a testator needs to take account of a wide range of possible scenarios at death, to work out how best to satisfy the needs of his or her dependants, and (in some cases) to consider the impact of taxation on the beneficiaries. Somewhat paradoxically perhaps, planning in all these senses may operate to curtail the very individualism which testamentary freedom supports and (especially if professional advice is sought) to obscure the testator's own untutored views about the ways in which property should be transmitted.

Who makes a will? When are 'last' wills made?

In this section the questions 'Who makes a will? When are wills made?' are examined using the data from our study of wills and national data on death, probate, and taxation. In respect of much of these data, including our own, the questions can only be addressed to 'last' wills for reasons which we have already explained. The answers illuminate wider questions relating to the reasons for making a will and the part which will-making plays in the testator's life.

The question of who makes a will is an important one, given that only a minority of the population does so. As we indicated in chapter 1, only 30 per cent of those who die aged over 18 leave a will which is admitted to probate. This figure has remained remarkably constant between 1959 and 1989, the period covered by the wills study. Over the same period, the percentage of formally administered intestacies has halved so that only one in ten adult deaths results in a grant of letters of administration. Formal administration is rarely necessary in the case of very small estates. The decline in formal intestacies without any growth in probate suggests that those dying intestate whilst owning considerable amounts of property is declining but that will-making is not increasing. However, surveys carried out for the Law Commission, in 1971 (Todd and Jones, 1972) and 1988 (Law Commission, 1989) indicated that the proportions of the public who have made a will or intend to do so have both increased over this period. It may be too early for any changes to be observed in the probate statistics. An alternative explanation is that will-making is viewed as a socially responsible activity and this may have exaggerated the positive response. Even if will-making is increasing, this may not lead to an increase in probated wills if the proportion of will-makers who die leaving little property and whose estates are consequently distributed informally is also increasing.

The proportions of adult men and women in the population is roughly equal but it has sometimes been suggested that men are more likely to make wills than women. A 1971 survey indicated a higher proportion of married men made wills than their wives (24 per cent compared with 10 per cent) (Todd and Jones, 1972: 33). Our own study suggests that roughly equal numbers of men and women made wills which were admitted to probate. Although there were slightly more wills made by women (417) than made by men (383) in the sample, the difference is not significant. However, these data are not directly comparable with the Todd and Jones study, in that we were not making direct comparisons between married couples.

The median age and life expectancy of our will-making sample differs from the population as a whole, both for women and men. Using the age at death as the basis of comparison, the median age at death of our will-makers was 72.6 years in 1959 and 77.1 years in 1989. The parallel figures for women are 78.6 years and 80.2 years. Figure 3.1 makes a comparison for each of our study years of the age at death in the adult population and the age at death of testators in our wills sample for that year. Those who make wills tend to be older at death than the population as a whole but the differences between men and women will-makers seem to reflect differences in the male and female populations as a whole. There appears to be less difference between age at death for women will-makers and all women, but this is not statistically significant. Similarly, the deaths of male will-makers appear slightly more concentrated than those of all men and women will-makers, with an inter-quartile range of approximately sixteen years, a pattern which is clearly observed if the four years of the sample are analysed separately.

The older age of will-makers may reflect their greater prosperity and higher social class compared with the population as a whole; improved life expectancy amongst such groups is well known (Townsend and Davidson, 1982: 51–6). Unfortunately the wills give no basis for making systematic social class comparisons because very few testators record their occupation in the will. A possible alternative

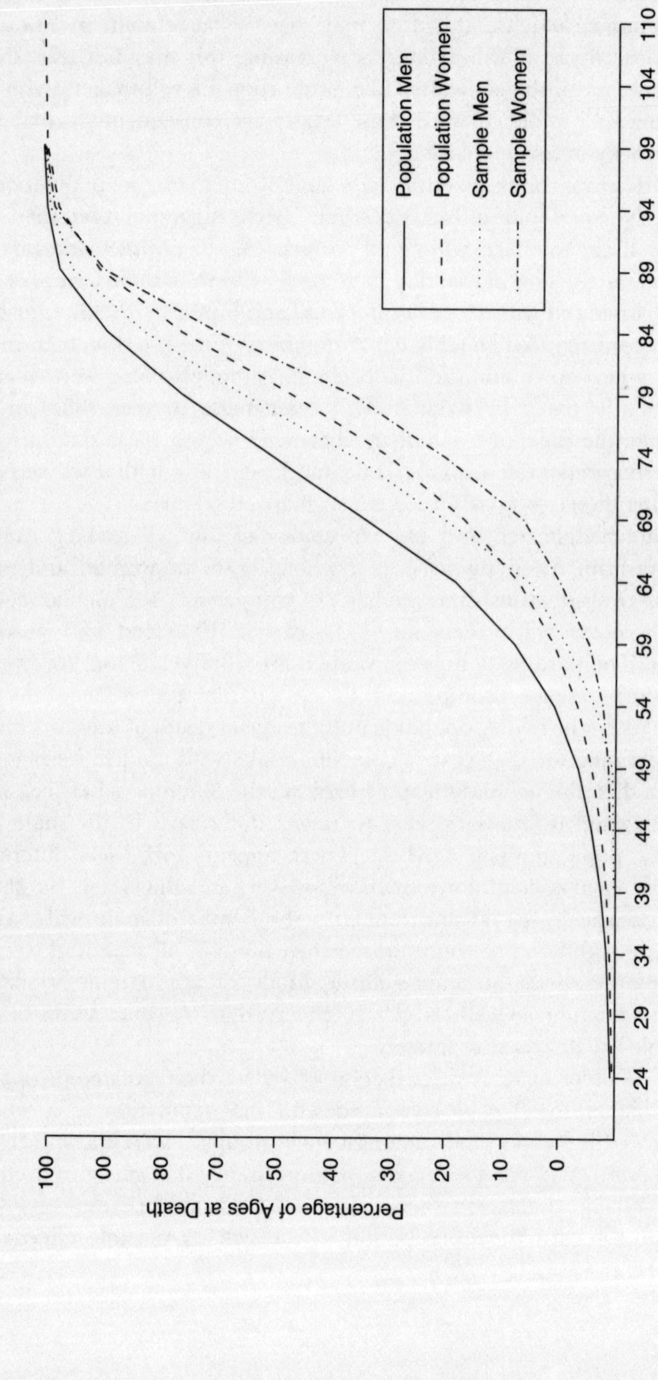

FIG. 3.1. Age at death—population of England and Wales and testators in wills sample compared

explanation is that those who live longer have had more time to contemplate death and greater experience of death within their own social network, and therefore have had more prompts to make a will.

As we indicated in chapter 1, the marital status of will-makers in the sample is more difficult to discern because testators frequently make no explicit reference to this. Men and women appear to differ in the way they describe themselves and are described by professionals in their wills. No men were identified as bachelors whereas 63 women were labelled spinsters, almost all in professionally made wills. Table 3.1 illustrates the marital status of the men and women in the sample, categorised in the ways described in chapter 1. Although the presumed single/divorced/widowed category is almost equally divided between men and women, a far higher proportion of the women were not married when their last will was drafted. Thirty-six per cent of the women were widowed and 15 per cent were spinsters; only 17 per cent were married at the time of making their last will. The very small proportion of those described explicitly as divorced may be explained by the reluctance of the individuals to be described in this way and the comparatively low divorce rates for those born before 1920 (i.e. the majority of the sample testators).

It is not possible to make comparisons with the total population because our testators' marital status at death is unknown. We cannot therefore state whether married people are more or less likely to make

TABLE 3.1. *Marital Status of will-makers × Gender*

	Men		Women		Total	
	N	%	N	%	N	%
Spinster/bachelor	0	–	63	15	63	8
Married	224	58	72	17	296	37
Widowed	18	5	150	36	168	21
Divorced	3	1	0	–	3	<1
Presumed single/ divorced/widowed	118	31	104	25	222	28
Status unknown	20	5	28	7	48	6
Total	383	100	417	100	800	100*

* *Note*: In this table, as with all others presented in this book, percentages are rounded up following the normal conventions. This can result in a total in excess of 100%.

wills than those never married, though the Law Commission survey did suggest this (Law Commission, 1989: 32). Although marriage would generally necessitate a new will because an existing one would be revoked, currently neither divorce nor widowhood have this effect.[1] Professionally drafted wills make allowance for the death of beneficiaries, thereby precluding the need for a new will, and the Administration of Justice Act 1982 operates to revoke gifts to, and the appointment as executor of, a spouse who is subsequently divorced. The elapse of time between will-making and dying, and the stage of life when wills are made, both make it likely that a substantial proportion of those married when their will was drafted would have died as widows or widowers.

Inheritance is frequently discussed in terms of wealth but this does not seem appropriate for the relatively modest amounts of property passed by the majority of wills in the first three years of the study. The median values of estates for the years 1959, 1969, and 1979 are shown in table 3.2. Exact figures were not available for 1989 because the Inland Revenue no longer required detailed accounts for estates of less than £100,000. Inflation, especially the marked increase in house values in the late 1980s, is reflected in the size of estates for 1989 with 96 per cent exceeding £40,000 and 21.5 per cent exceeding £100,000. The range of values is wide, with the largest estates exceeding £100,000 for the first three sample years and £1 million in 1989, and the smallest estates being under £100 in 1959 and 1969. The majority of the estates in the study were below the threshold for tax. Most were also within the limit of the spouse's statutory legacy for cases of intestacy where the deceased left no children.

There were differences in the values of men's and women's estates, and between the estates of single and married people. Such differences have been observed in earlier studies of larger estates (Diamond Commission, 1977) and in Scotland (Munro, 1988). The median size of estates was significantly lower for women in 1959 and 1969. Higher percentages of women left estates in the lowest quartile of values; women were under-represented in the highest quartile, but this difference was less marked except in 1959. The median value of single

[1] A paper produced by the Law Commission in 1993 recommends a change to the Wills Act 1837, so that following a divorce a former spouse would be treated—for inheritance purposes—as if s/he had died on the date of the divorce (Law Commission, 1993a). A provision to implement this recommendation has been included in the Law Reform (Succession) Bill introduced in the 1994/5 Parliamentary Session.

TABLE 3.2. *Estate size (various measures) × Year of probate*

Year		1959	1969	1979	1989
Median all estates	£	1,904	2,981	14,571	n.a.
Median men	£	2,161	3,432	14,489	n.a.
Median women	£	1,420	2,877	14,546	n.a.
Percentage of estates:					
above £100,000	%	0.5	0.5	1.5	21.5
below tax threshold	%	65	63.5/82*	76	85.5
less than lower statutory legacy	%	76.5	79.5	76	n.a.
greater than or equal to higher statutory legacy	%	7	5.5	6.5	13.5
Median estate: unmarried	£	1,690	2,865	13,326	n.a.
Median estate: married	£	2,520	3,566	15,793	n.a.
Median estate: widows	£	2,366	3,352	17,182	n.a.

* *Note*: lower figure represents tax rate prior to 1969 budget.

testators' estates appears significantly lower than that for married people but it should be noted that there were more women in this group. The median for widows was greater than that for all women in each of the first three sample years, reflecting the importance of inherited property for elderly women's wealth. In contrast, married women were the poorest group, except in 1979 where the median for spinsters' estates was lowest at £14,204. The change in fortunes of single, widowed, and married women may reflect changes in the way property, particularly house property, is held in the family and the growth of pensions and life assurance benefits for widows. The pattern of increasing wealth with age observed in the earlier studies is not apparent in this study, but this may be due to the distribution of housing wealth, as Munro (1988: 427) suggests in relation to Scotland.

The range of estate sizes can also give some clues about the question of intestacy. Figure 3.2 compares the size of estates in the wills sample with Inland Revenue statistics for size of estates: the latter include formally administered intestacies. There appear to be no significant differences between the two groups, suggesting that intestacy occurs proportionally throughout the full range of estate values

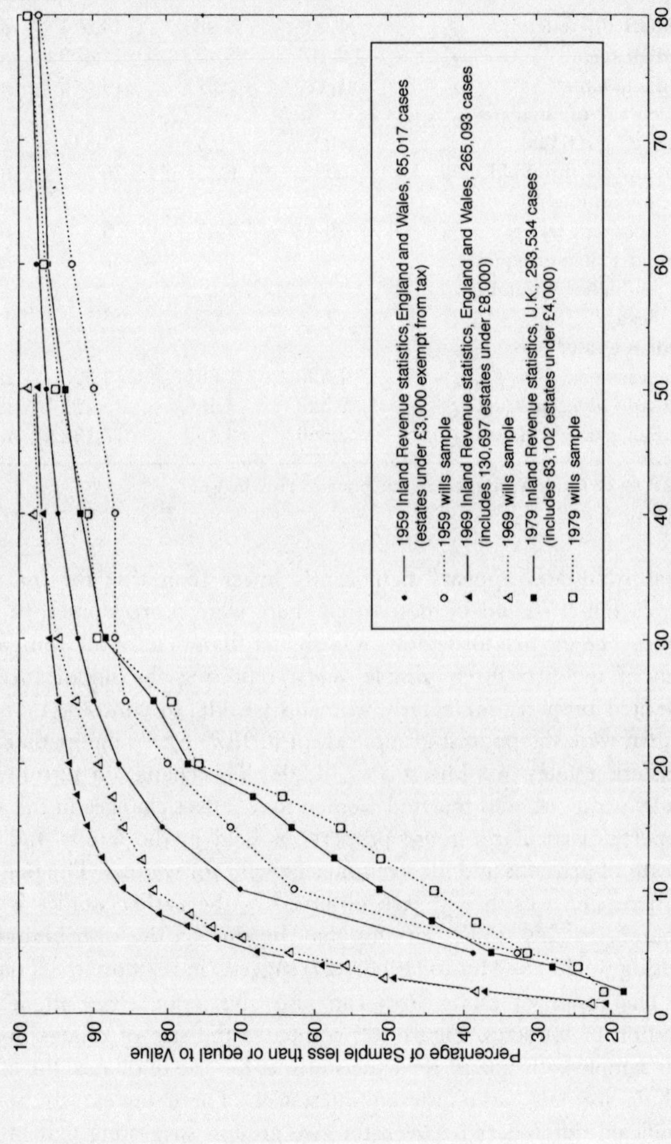

FIG. 3.2. Size of estate—wills sample and Inland Revenue statistics compared

rather than being concentrated amongst smaller estates. Although owning property provides an incentive to make a will, there are some with substantial assets who fail to do so. The decline in the number of formally administered estates between 1959 and 1989 indicates such failure is becoming less common.

In summary then, we can say that women and men are equally likely to make wills though, in so far as marital status can be discerned from wills, female will-makers are less likely than men to be married at the time of making their 'last' will. In terms of wealth, the decision to make a will is spread quite broadly amongst the population, not confined just to those who have significant assets to bequeath. However, the greater life expectancy of will-makers, by comparison with the population as a whole, suggests that they may be drawn more from higher socio-economic groups (even though, in some cases, they have relatively little to bequeath).

What can the wills sample tell us about the circumstances which prompt people to make (or perhaps to remake) their will? Given that many people do not do so, it seems reasonable to ask what prompts some people to overcome what is widely seen as a 'kind of superstitious reluctance' (Comyn and Johnson, 1970: 4) to make a will, because of the need to contemplate one's own death and its consequences.

One clue to the circumstances which prompt will-making can come from the date on the will. All wills are dated to avoid disputes if more than one is found. This information and information about testators' date of death and age at death makes it possible to explore the stage in their life when testators made their last will. Table 3.3 shows how long before death the sample wills were made. The median was just under five years with 11 per cent made less than a year before death and 25 per cent made over ten years earlier. A third of the 59 codicils were

TABLE 3.3. *Length of time between writing will and testator's death*

	N	%
Less than 1 year	86	11
1 year or more but less than 2	113	14
2 years or more but less than 5	188	24
5 years or more but less than 10	217	27
10 years or more	196	25
Total	800	100

made within a year of death and a fifth within a year of the original will, suggesting that, for those who used codicils, change as death approached was only slightly more common than second thoughts shortly after the will was made. No significant differences were observed between male or female testators, nor over the four sample years of the study, despite major changes in the law which might have made reviewing an earlier will more important for those dying after the Inheritance (Provision for Family and Dependants) Act 1975 or the Administration of Justice Act 1982. The proportions of home-made and professional wills was also similar both for wills with codicils and those without. There is therefore no evidence either that making one's own will is a 'death bed' activity or that lawyers have successfully encouraged clients to review their wills regularly.

The age of the testators when their will was made ranged from 26 years to 97 years with a median of 69 years for men and 73 years for women, slightly below the average life expectancy for each. The age distribution of men and women is illustrated in figure 3.3. The age distribution for men is wider than for women but 50 per cent of each group is found over a sixteen-year period, covering the ages of 61 to 77 years for men and 65 to 81 years for women. This demonstrates that making one's last will is predominantly an activity undertaken by the elderly. Slight peaks can be observed in the number of men making wills at the age of 65, the male retirement age, and 76, but there is no similar pattern for women. The median age for making codicils was 77 years. A high proportion of wills of those who died in 1959 was made when the testator was under 50, some of which would have been made during war-time, but there was otherwise little difference in the age distribution of testators over the four decades. There was little difference between the age distribution of those who used solicitors and those who made their own wills, except that a higher proportion of those making their own wills were under the age of 60 years and nobody over the age of 90 made a will without professional assistance.

The age of will-makers makes it unlikely that they had minor children, a view reinforced by the absence of guardianship appointments in these wills. Rather, it suggests that their own age and the deaths of relatives (a third of women had already been widowed) are likely to have encouraged them to contemplate their own mortality. For the majority of men but less than a fifth of women, the context for this was a subsisting marriage where any children were already adults. It is also likely that wills were made after most of the testators' wealth had

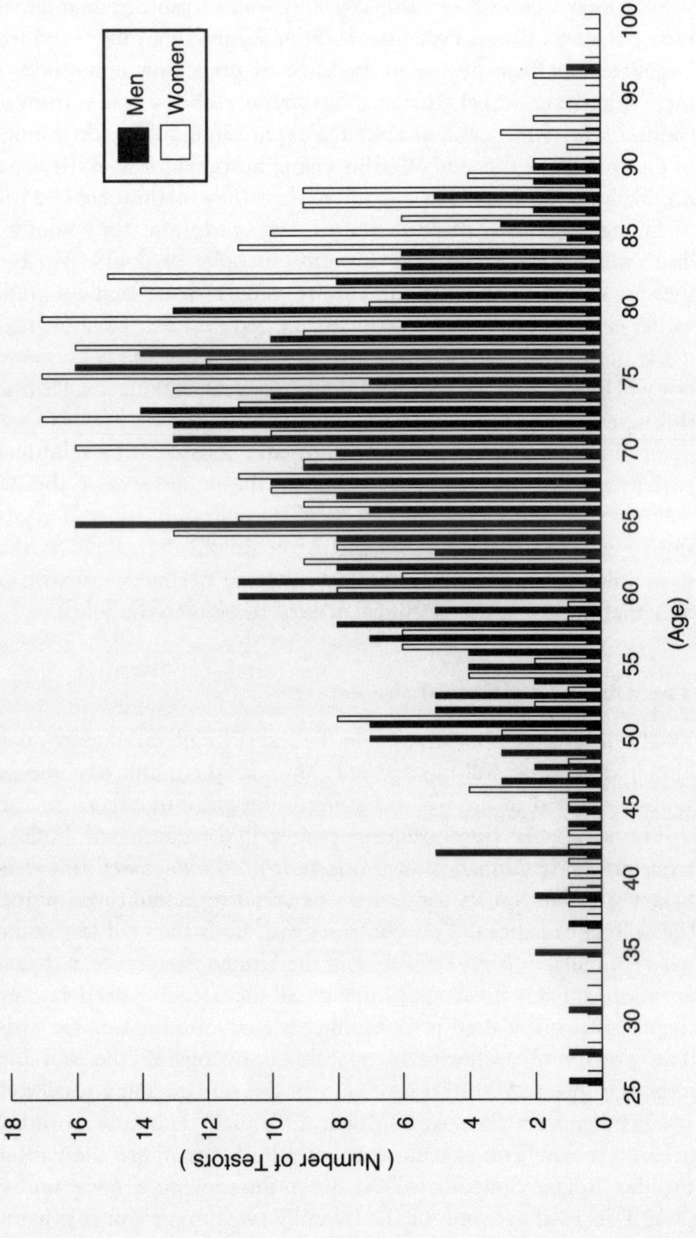

FIG. 3.3. Age when will made—men and women

been acquired. The majority of testators were beyond retirement age so real increases in their assets, if any, would come from inheritance rather than earnings. Previous research suggests that inherited wealth largely comes from people in the same or preceding generations with men inheriting largely from their parents and women from their spouses (Harbury, 1962; Diamond Commission, 1977). Only one-fifth of the women in the study had surviving husbands; few of the testators are likely to have had parents alive when they made their last will.

Though our own study demonstrates clearly that the making of a 'last' will occurs in old age for most people, of course we cannot thereby conclude that will-making in general is an activity confined to the elderly. As we have indicated, we have no way of knowing how many of our sample had made previous wills. Any will is potentially a last will but an understanding of the reasons for making a will obtained through studying probated wills may under-estimate the role of wills in protecting the testator's young family and consolidating relationships earlier in life. It may also over-estimate the importance of the monetary value of the estate because smaller estates are more likely to be distributed informally. A fuller picture could only be gained by including earlier wills (and others not admitted to probate) and with more information about the circumstances of those who die intestate.

The administration of the estate

Finally, in this chapter, we turn to the last stage of will-making, namely anticipating what will happen once one has died, and how the provisions contained in the will are going to be put into effect.

The system of administering estates in England and Wales and securing the transmission of property from the deceased to the beneficiary is reliant on the deceased's personal representatives, named in the will as executors. This contrasts with both the civil law countries where the heirs play a key role and the United States where the courts are more actively involved. On death all the testator's property vests in the executors; it is their responsibility to carry out the testator's wishes. The executors' authority is established by having the will proved although this may not be necessary in the case of many small estates. In all but a very few cases (Miller, 1977: 79) probate is an administrative process. The executors are required to produce the will at the Probate Registry, a court office, swear the executors' oath, and complete a detailed account for the Inland Revenue. Assistance is available

TABLE 3.4. *Number of executors × Whether named executors are professionals*

	Sole executor		Multiple executors		Total
	N	%	N	%	
Non-professional only	358	83	240	65	598
Professional only	71	17	43	12	114
Both professional and non-professional	0	0	87	23	87
Total	429	100	270	100	799

Note: this analysis omits one will where no executor was named. Most of the 'professionals' were solicitors.

to personal applicants in each probate registry, but probate is sought by solicitors in about 85 per cent of cases each year (*Judicial Statistics*, 1989). In the majority of these cases, solicitors are acting on behalf of lay executors. Even where the grant of probate is obtained without a solicitor, the work of administering the estate may be passed on to one.

Technically the winding up of the estate is under the supervision of the court but effectively this means only that there are established processes for challenging the actions of the executors which include imposing personal liability for improper action. No special skills are required from executors, but the law assumes that the testator will select people who can be trusted with the task and who are able and willing to perform it. Executors can only be compelled to distribute property a year after the death, but speedy administration may be achieved by choosing executors with an incentive to complete the task.

There is no limit to the number of executors, though of course the appointment of more than one may act as a safeguard against dishonesty or incompetency and increase the chances that there will be someone able to undertake the task. Just over half the testators in our sample appointed only one executor, only 5 per cent appointed more than two. In about a quarter of the wills a professional, usually a solicitor, was appointed (see table 3.4). Eighty-seven of these were appointed to act alongside lay people. The effect of such a joint appointment is to ensure that the estate is administered professionally by solicitors chosen by the testator. It will almost always be the solicitors who have drafted the will who obtain the lucrative probate work, either in this way or following instructions from a lay executor who has collected the original will from their office. Administration may be facilitated by being done by someone responsible for the drafting of the will; some of the solicitors interviewed in our study commented that they felt more secure if wills drafted in the firm were probated through the firm (Masson, 1994). Such views may reflect the relative economic importance of probate work to solicitors' firms rather than concern that wills might have been poorly drafted.

In our wills sample there was a strong likelihood that lay executors would also be named as beneficiaries, except in the case of in-laws (see table 3.5). In addition, 198 lay executors (18 per cent) were substitute beneficiaries. It appears that many testators selected executors from amongst their beneficiaries. This suggests that only where there was no one suitable or where the solicitor's influence was strong would they look to professionals or kin who did not benefit from the will. Presumably beneficiaries could be relied on to complete the task in order to obtain their share. The provision of a gift could be seen as creating a moral obligation which made it difficult for the person not to accept the appointment. Spouses and children were the kin most commonly

TABLE 3.5. *Non-professional executors: relationship to testator and whether beneficiary*

	Total of this kin type appointed executors	Proportion of appointees who are sole executors		Proportion of appointees who are also beneficiaries	
		N	%	N	%
Spouse	211	144	68	211	100
Child	309	86	28	303	98
Child's spouse	29	7	24	14	45
Sibling	82	33	40	67	82
Sibling's spouse	15	2	13	8	53
Niece/nephew	80	24	28	76	95
Aunt/uncle/ cousin	8	1	13	5	63
Friend/ neighbour	39	16	41	23	59
Total	781	313		707	

Note: this table excludes executors whose relationship to testator is unclear. It includes the first two executors named, but excludes any others if there were more than two.

selected as executors, but only six children and no spouses were chosen without also receiving gifts (see table 3.5). Where non-beneficiaries were chosen as executors they were more likely to be friends or relations by marriage. Some of these will have benefited indirectly from the will since, out of 152 non-beneficiaries appointed, 59 were the spouse, child or grandchild of a beneficiary. For some non-beneficiaries receipt of a gift by a spouse may be viewed as receiving it personally; in the Todd and Jones study two-thirds of wives and three-quarters of husbands stated that they considered property they inherited to belong to the household (Todd and Jones, 1972: 26). In a few cases where the executor was not the beneficiary a small sum was set aside as a payment for him or her. Thus only a small minority of lay individuals were expected to undertake the task without some reward.

The majority of executors (57 per cent) were from the first generation below the testator. An obvious reason for this is that such people were more likely than those of the same generation to be alive and able to take on the task when the testator died. However only four executors appeared to have been selected from the second generation, namely grandchildren and great nephews, and only one from the generation above the testator, an aunt.

The other large group of executors were the testators' spouses. Where spouses were named as executors the majority were appointed sole executors. In most of these cases no question of supervising the distribution of the estate would have arisen because the spouse was also the sole beneficiary of the estate. Only just over a quarter of children who were appointed as executors were named as the sole executor (table 3.5). This, perhaps, reflects a general tendency to treat all children on equal terms in wills (see chapter 5), which would suggest joint appointment of all the children unless the testator had a special reason to be selective. Around 40 per cent of siblings and friends named as executors were appointed alone. These relatively high proportions may reflect the degree of trust felt by the testators or the view that there were no other suitable persons with whom the task could be shared.

There were proportionately more women than men appointed sole executor and these gender differences are even more marked for spouses (table 3.6). In general almost all female executors were also beneficiaries (94 per cent) whereas the corresponding proportion for men is lower (76 per cent). Thus, despite the fact that most executors can be expected to instruct professionals to do the work, it seems that

TABLE 3.6. *Gender of non-professional executors × Other features*

	Total	Proportion who are sole executors		Proportion of sole executors who are spouses		Proportion who are beneficiaries	
		N	%	N	%	N	%
Male executor	522	161	31	57	11	396	76
Female executor	422	199	47	154	37	397	94
Total	944	360	38	211	22	793	84

Note: if there are more than two non-professional executors named, only the first two are included in the analysis.

this role remains one which is felt to belong to men and appropriate only for women where it largely amounts to managing the transmission of assets from the estate to themselves.

Concluding remarks

In this chapter we have begun to answer some of the research questions which we posed at the end of chapter 1, in particular our first set of questions: how do people approach the process of will-making? under what circumstances do people make a will? how common is it to take legal advice? how common is it to make changes in an existing will?

Our general conclusions are that will-making can certainly be seen as a 'planned' activity. Our own sample of wills suggests it is almost always done following a conscious decision, not on the spur of the moment, and rarely is it a death-bed activity. However, the types of 'planning' involved for most people essentially concern making provision for their dependants and ensuring that the distribution of their assets takes place according to their own wishes. Though data from wills cannot be conclusive on this point, we find little evidence that tax planning—much discussed in a professional, legal context—plays a part for most will-makers.

The circumstances under which people make their 'last' will typically is in old age and probably, for women in particular, following the death of a spouse. Thus most people have fairly up-to-date wills when they die, though about a quarter have a will which is more than ten years old. There is little evidence that lawyers have been successful in getting people to review their will regularly; certainly the use of codicils is rare. However, more generally, professionals are important in will-making. Most people do consult a professional, usually a solicitor, when writing their will and the tendency to do so has increased over time.

Wills are made by a wide cross-section of the population, on the evidence of our study. Men and women are equally likely to make a will, and will-making is certainly not confined to the wealthy. Many people make a will even though they have only very modest assets. It therefore makes sense to ask the other research questions which we posed in chapter 1, concerning the choices which people make about the disposition of their property. We can now do this in the confidence that our wills sample contains not simply a group of wealthy individuals but a cross-section drawn from ordinary families.

4 First Choices: Patterns of Bequeathing

We move now to explore the content of bequeathing choices in our random sample of 800 wills. Since our particular focus is on family relationships, and what wills can tell us about these in the context of inheritance, we have used our wills to explore in some detail the relationships between testators and beneficiaries. As we indicated in chapter 1, we are trying to understand how people's concept of 'family' gets defined in this context. Our sample also enables us to explore whether these patterns have changed over our four sample years.

In this chapter we will examine the basic patterns of bequeathing, looking first at who gets included as beneficiaries, then at the forms in which bequests are made. In chapter 5 we put the 'who' and the 'what' patterns together in an attempt to understand the principles which lie behind people's bequeathing decisions. Both chapters 4 and 5 focus on first choices, that is, on the people named in the wills as the direct recipients of gifts. In our analysis we refer to these as 'first line' beneficiaries and bequests. In chapter 6 we examine the question of substitution, that is, bequests made only if the first choice of beneficiary should predecease the testator. These three chapters, taken together, enable us to explore the complex patterns of bequeathing revealed in our sample of 800 wills.

Points of comparison with other research

From this point onwards, where possible, we will make comparisons between our own data and earlier studies of inheritance. However, there are some limitations here which derive in part from differences of focus. We want to draw four particular contrasts here, which also enable us to clarify some points about how we have handled our own data.

The first point concerns the concept of 'beneficiaries'. In the past, researchers have been addressing different questions from ours, focusing on the issues inheritance raises at a macro level, namely the impact of inheritance on the distribution of wealth in general (Diamond Commission, 1977; Horsman, 1978) or housing wealth in particular (Munro, 1988; Hamnett, Harmer, and Williams, 1991). As a consequence, previous researchers have developed a unit of analysis referred to as the 'main beneficiary'. For Hamnett and his colleagues such an analysis meant the exclusion of certain beneficiaries: 'recipients of minor legacies and beneficiaries of small proportions of the estate where the bulk had been left to others were left out of the analysis' (Hamnett, Harmer, and Williams, 1991: 86).

However, our study is more concerned with what patterns of will-making can tell us about how the disposal of assets reflects and honours relationships between kin and non-kin, across all ranges of estate size. In order to address the kind of research questions and issues we outlined above, all beneficiaries mentioned in a will potentially are of interest, no matter whether they receive the major portion of the estate or are simply bequeathed a cash gift of £10. So our first point of departure from previous studies is that all data contained in the will are important to our analysis.

A further reason for departing from the main beneficiary as a unit of analysis relates to the difficulties of drawing conclusions about monetary value of bequests from the content of the will. Working from wills data alone, it is often difficult to be certain who would be the main beneficiary of the estate since the monetary value of specific bequests such as jewellery or shares is impossible to determine. The Diamond Commission (1977) supplemented wills data with information from the Capital Taxes Office in order to develop more accurate valuations of specific bequests which enabled them to measure the actual volume of wealth bequeathed to particular beneficiaries (including some lifetime transfers). Other studies have relied on educated guesses. The problematic nature of such an approach is acknowledged in the Hamnett study:

> In certain cases it proved difficult to decide which had been the major beneficiary of the estate. Wills often state that particular assets are going to one beneficiary, the remainder to another. It was usually possible to decide on the basis of the estate's total value and the nature of the specified assets who had been the major beneficiary and classify the case accordingly. (Hamnett, Harmer, and Williams, 1991: 86).

In our own study, based on wills data alone, we did not feel it possible to make accurate guesses.

Our analysis therefore, unlike previous research, includes the full range of beneficiaries and does not attempt to guess who actually receives the most valuable portion of the estate. Though earlier studies have drawn certain conclusions about family commitments implicit in wills, our particular approach enables us look at aspects of this which have not been explored in previous research. Our data will allow us to problematize the notion of bequeathing to the family, enabling us to examine for example, the treatment of affines and step-relatives, who figure very little in studies focused on the 'main beneficiary'.

The second point at which we depart from earlier studies is that we are interested in the form in which bequests are made. In the past, research based on wills data has been predominantly concerned with who gets mentioned as beneficiaries. But the question of what *type* of bequests are made has remained largely unexplored. Our own work links these two types of question together in order to investigate whether any clear principles appear to get incorporated into the way in which estates are divided, and whether certain types of property are seen to be appropriate to certain types of beneficiary. Though the question of the form in which property gets passed on might seem of limited interest, especially in families with modest assets, in fact it emerges as a crucial factor in our own analysis, as we show later in this chapter.

Third, our analysis is different from previous research in the way in which we treat gifts made *inter vivos* (see chapters 2 and 3). In common with all studies based on wills, we have the problem that we cannot know what gifts have passed outside the will. In other research concerned primarily with the transmission of wealth, the absence of information about gifts *inter vivos* has led to a concern that wills data may in fact under-represent the amount of wealth passing by as much as 15–20 per cent (Horsman, 1975; Diamond Commission, 1977). In our own study we are less concerned with this particular issue, but more concerned with how the absence of information about gifts *inter vivos* might influence our interpretation of the will itself, and the ways in which testators are acknowledging family relationships.

One example of this would be cases in which people of the same kin type are treated differently by being left unequal shares of the same sort of gift (see chapter 5 for further discussion of differential treatment). This would be the case in a will which bequeathed a cash gift to a daughter of £3,000 whilst containing a bequest of £2,000 to a son. At face value the testator appears to be treating the children unequally but this may not necessarily be the intention. For example, it could represent an intention to even out gifts made to children during the testator's lifetime. We have an example of such a process in the will of Thomas Pounder, written in 1955, in which he bequeathed at substitution: 'five hundred pounds for my son Frank Pounder in order to equalise a gift of five hundred pounds made during my life to my said son Mark Rush'. Thomas then goes on to divide the residue equally between his sons. This is in fact the only will in our sample which explicitly indicates such a motivation for treating beneficiaries of the same kin type differently, but there may be more of which we are unaware. Without such explicit acknowledgement it would be impossible to detect the impact of other property transfers on the disposal of assets in a will. For this research it is important to acknowledge the potential effect of one set of wealth transfers, those made during a person's lifetime, on plans to dispose of assets at death. This is in contrast to the concerns of previous research which simply wished to add lifetime transfers of wealth together with those made at death in order to gain a more accurate overall picture of wealth transmission.

Finally, because of our particular focus, our study maintains an interest in people who are *not* left gifts as well as those who are. For example, whilst a testator may appear, on the evidence of the will, to be treating his or her children equally, if we were to discover that the testator had another child who did not benefit from the will, the equality of the will would be in question. The particular research questions which we are addressing lead us to conceptualise this facet of the wills data in a rather different way from that adopted in previous research. Of course it also provides us with a particular problem in interpreting our data, since we can have no knowledge of the existence of relatives who simply are not mentioned in the will. In principle this information is available in public records but searching for it, even in a small number of cases, would be impossibly time-consuming and we have not attempted to do so. However, the wills themselves do give some clues about relatives who have not received a gift, as we show below.

In drawing these four points of contrast between our own and previous research, we have also highlighted certain points at which we need to be cautious about the interpretation of our wills data. Bearing these points in mind, we now move to our exploration of bequeathing patterns in our sample of 800 wills, looking first at beneficiaries, then at bequests.

Beneficiaries: who benefits from wills?

We begin our discussion of beneficiaries named in wills by outlining some of the basic patterns: how many? who are they? from which generations (relative to the testator)? Some basic patterns found in the wills are summarised in table 4.1. The significance of each of the items will become apparent as our discussion develops.

How important are kin?

Bequests are not always made to individuals, although almost all wills do mention individual beneficiaries (796 wills, out of 800). A much smaller percentage of testators include at least one bequest to a group of beneficiaries (6 per cent, 48 wills) (see table 4.1). It may not always be clear how many individuals are included in group bequests since the testator may simply write '£100 to each of my grandchildren alive at my death'. In such bequests each grandchild is given a fixed amount of money but in some wills the amount to be left to the *group* is fixed, so that the amount each member receives is dependent on the number in the group who survive the testator. The groups included in the wills tend to be from descendent generations. Indeed the further we move down the generations, the more likely are group bequests. The exception to this is nieces and nephews who are as likely as siblings (that is, as their parental generation) to be included in a group bequest. As we shall see later, this is perhaps explained by the particular treatment which nieces and nephews receive in wills.

On average, each will mentions 3.5 beneficiaries with no significant change over our four sample years. It is common practice for testators to state their relationship to the beneficiaries whom they name in their will. Indeed the relationship was specified for 70 per cent of the 3,575 individuals mentioned in our sample of wills: in most of our wills therefore we were able to categorise the identity of every beneficiary. We were unable to identify at least one beneficiary's relationship in 18 per cent of our wills . Only 32 wills, from the total of 800, consisted entirely of beneficiaries whose relationship to the testator could not be distinguished (see table 4.2), although in some cases we know that they are relatives because they have the same surname as the testator. These cases of 'kin, relationship unclear' appear in other wills also; a total of 4 per cent contains at least one beneficiary categorised in this way.

In our sample, 735 testators (92%) named at least one relative amongst their first choice of beneficiaries. Seventeen per cent named at least one non-relative and only 9 per cent named a charity or other

TABLE 4.1. *Bequeathing at first line: basic patterns*

N = 800	N	%
Individual and 'group' bequests:		
Includes at least one named, individual beneficiary	796	100
Includes at least one 'group' of beneficiaries	48	6
Relatives and others:		
Names at least one relative as a first choice beneficiary (blood, step or affine)	735	92
Names at least one non-relative as a first choice beneficiary	138	17
Names at least one organisation as a first choice beneficiary	70	9
Types of relatives named:		
Includes a spouse	294	37
Includes at least one child	291	36
Includes spouse plus child(ren)	63	8
Includes a grandchild	93	12
Includes a sibling	146	18
Includes a niece/nephew	137	17
Includes at least one beneficiary from: spouse, child, grandchild, sibling, niece/nephew	709	88
Includes at least one beneficiary from: affine, step-relative, great-grandchild, great-niece/nephew, cousin	121	15
Type of will:		
Total estate wills	414	52
Composite wills	386	48
Inclusion of spouse in different types of will:		
Total estate will bequeathing all to spouse	196	25
Total estate will including spouse plus at least one other beneficiary	5	<1
Total estate will *not* including a spouse	215	27
Composite will including a spouse	95	12
Composite will *not* including a spouse	291	36

Note: on this table, as with all others presented in this book, percentages are rounded up following normal conventions. Thus numbers slightly less than the total of 800 appear as 100%.

organisation. Because of the small number of organisations named, and because our particular interest is in bequests to individuals, particularly kin, we have not developed further our analysis of bequeathing to charities.

TABLE 4.2. *Patterns of bequests to selected groups*

	Total estate wills		Composite wills		All wills	
N = 800	N	%	N	%	N	%
Spouse	199	48	95	25	294	37
Blood relative	175	42	338	88	513	64
Affine	8	2	75	19	83	10
Step-relative	3	0.7	13	3	16	2
Other kin	5	1	38	10	43	5
Non-kin	17	4	121	31	138	17
Unidentified beneficiaries	32	8	115	29	147	18

FIG. 4.1. Exclusive presence of kin and non-kin as first line beneficiaries × Type of will

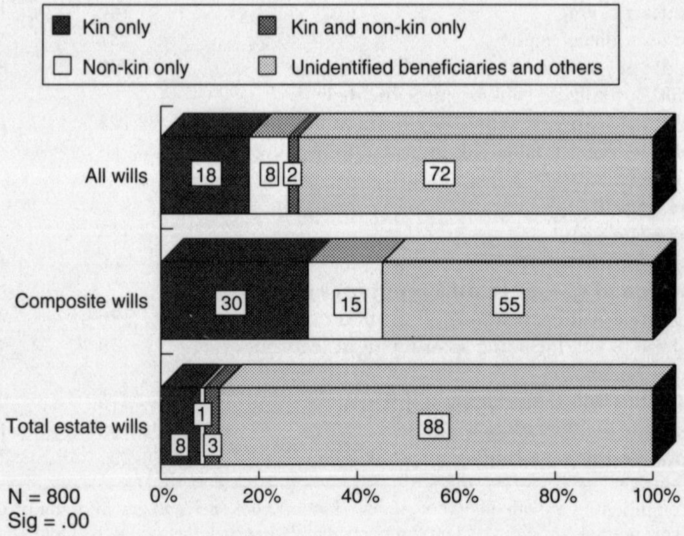

Note: the 'sig.' amount given here, and in certain other figures and tables, is an outcome of a Pearson chi-square test. As with all such tests, the meaning of this amount needs to be interpreted in the light of sample and cell size. The 'non-kin only' figure for 'Composite Wills' is less than 1% and is therefore not represented. 'Unidentified beneficiaries and others' refers to wills which have a beneficiary whose status we cannot identify, and other beneficiaries (including organizations).

From table 4.2 it is clear that the named relatives are more likely to be blood relatives than in-laws or step-relatives. Non-kin appear in less than one-fifth of wills. When we look at combinations of kin and non-kin in wills, almost three-quarters of our sample leave exclusively to kin. We can identify only 2 per cent of wills in our sample which bequeathed everything to non-kin. The top line of figure 4.1 gives the relevant data. (The bottom two lines refer to our division of wills into 'total estate' and 'composite' (see chapter 3): we discuss the significance of these variations later in this chapter). Our data show that bequeathing to kin clearly is the preferred way of distributing assets. At the simplest level therefore, our wills support the idea that will-makers in England do in fact favour family members in their bequeathing decisions despite the considerable freedom to bequeath which the law allows (see chapter 2).

At this point we can make some comparisons between our data and earlier research, though our figures have been calculated on a different basis for reasons which we explained above. Hamnett, Harmer, and Williams, whose sample covered a wide range of estate values taken from 1981 probate calendars, discovered that in 81 per cent of wills a relative was a main beneficiary (1991: table 5.5, p. 87). For Horsman (1978) the figure was higher at 86 per cent and interestingly the sample was of very high estates, all above £50,000 (probated in 1979). This raises interesting questions about the relationship between estate size and the likelihood of relatives as major beneficiaries. A re-analysis of the Hamnett figures (see table 4.3) shows that the medium-sized estates have the highest percentage of relatives as main beneficiaries, suggesting no simple linear relationship between estate size and the likelihood that beneficiaries will be relatives of the testator.

The Hamnett sample included a wide range of estate values which probably explains why a different picture emerges when we look at the results of the Diamond Commission (1977), which included only high value estates in its sample. The Diamond Commission also carried out a more sophisticated analysis of how much property beneficiaries received. By supplementing the wills data with information from the Capital Taxes Office, the Diamond Commission was able to calculate quite accurately the amount of wealth going to each beneficiary in a will, rather than making judgements about who was the main beneficiary. The data indicated that the proportion of disposable estate left to relatives varied inversely with the size of the estate. So that from estates over £500,000, 76 per cent of the disposable property (net estate) went to a relative, compared with 91 per cent in the case of

TABLE 4.3. *Analysis of relationship of major beneficiaries to testator × Total estate value, in data reported by Hamnett, Harmer, and Williams (1991)*

	Estate size											
	<£10,000		£10,000–<£25,000		£25,000–<£40,000		£40,000–<£60,000		£60,000–<£100,000		>£100,000	
	N	%	N	%	N	%	N	%	N	%	N	%
Relative(s) only (including spouse)	253	79	152	81	170	83	84	87	50	74	42	82
Others (including combinations of other categories)	21	7	10	5	20	10	6	6	6	9	4	8
No major beneficiary stated	35	11	18	10	11	5	6	6	8	12	4	8
Charity only	11	3	8	4	4	2	1	1	4	6	1	2
Total	320	100	188	100	205	100	97	100	68	100	51	100

Source: adapted from Table 5.5, *Safe as Houses: Housing Inheritance in Britain* by Hamnett, Harmer, and Williams, (1991). Reprinted with permission of the author and Paul Chapman Publishing Ltd., London.

estates with values between £15,000 and £50,000. The different results of the two studies may simply reflect the different estate sizes which they sampled. If the Diamond Commission had included the lower value estates found in the Hamnett study, the pattern may have been repeated.

In our own study it was clear that there is an inverse relationship between the size of estate and whether bequests go exclusively to kin. The pattern therefore is the same as Diamond, although we have to bear in mind that we were looking at exclusive bequests to kin rather than at kin who received the majority of the estate (see figure 4.2). The Diamond report noted a clear tendency for the relative value of property left to *non-kin* to increase with the size of the estate; non-kin

FIG. 4.2. Exclusive presence of kin and non-kin × Estate size
(Estate values have been divided into quartiles with value 1 the lowest.)

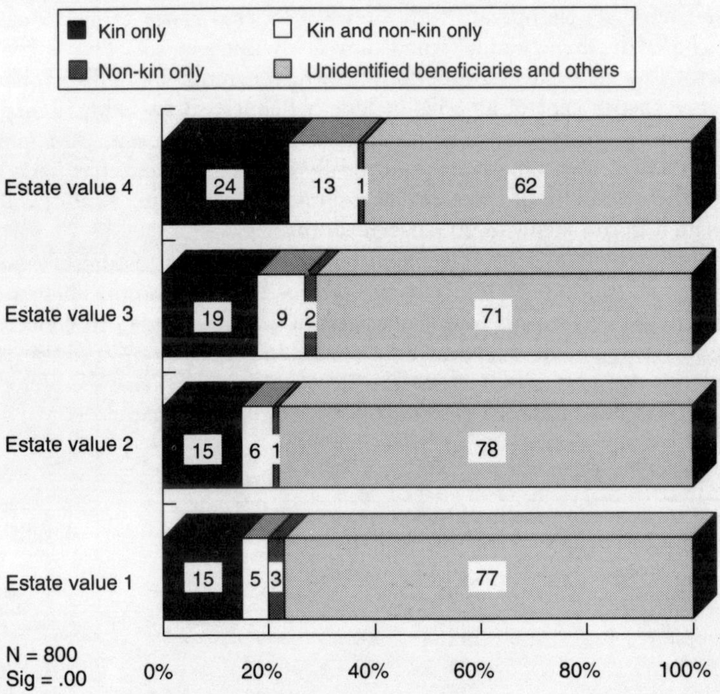

Note: the 'values' in this figure represent the four quartiles of estate values for each sample year, added together. Value 1 is the lowest quartile, value 4 is the highest.

accounted for 9 per cent of disposable estate bequeathed in the lowest-value estates compared with 25 per cent in the highest-value estates (Diamond Commission, 1977: table 83, p.171). Again we have no directly comparable data but it is interesting to note that high-value estates are most likely to contain bequests both to kin and non-kin in the same will, and the lowest-value estates are the least likely (figure 4.2).

Which kin? Which generations?

Kin therefore continue to be the major—often the exclusive—beneficiaries of wills, especially in estates of modest value. But *which* kin are the most likely to be named? On the surface, the answer to this question is unsurprising. The basic patterns are given in table 4.1. Eighty-eight per cent mention one or more of the following: spouse, child, grandchild, sibling, niece/nephew. This range has changed very little over time (significance 0.35), indicating that there are clear and consistent ideas about who should be included in a will. This suggests that most people operate with a fairly restricted range of individuals included in their 'family' when they are writing a will. This is confirmed by the smaller number of wills which mention more distant kin. Only 15 per cent of all wills include a bequest to an affine, a step-relative, a great-grandchild, great-niece/nephew or cousin. Although the change over time is not statistically significant, there has been a steady increase in the presence of distant kin from 14 per cent of wills written in the 1950s to 20 per cent in the 1980s.

The individual categories mentioned most often are spouses (37 per cent) and children (36 per cent) (see table 4.4, final column). These are precisely the kin with whose interests the law has tended to concern itself when it has sought to limit testamentary freedom and also in relation to intestacy. Of course the rules for the latter have themselves been based on patterns of bequeathing in wills (see chapter 2).

TABLE 4.4. *Kin included most frequently × Different types of will*

	Total estate wills		Composite wills		All wills	
	N	%	N	%	N	%
Spouse	199	48	95	25	294	37
Children	109	26	182	47	291	36
Grandchildren	6	1	87	23	93	12
Siblings	43	10	103	27	146	18
Niece/Nephews	21	5	116	30	137	17

However, it would be wrong to assume that the act of bequeathing is, in general, simply a matter of identifying one's closest kin and passing all one's property to that person or persons. In some cases it certainly seems to be like that. But the deeper one probes the more complex the picture becomes, as we shall show in the rest of this chapter and those which follow. We can begin to see this point if we ask the simple question: from which generations are beneficiaries drawn?

One common-sense understanding of inheritance is that it is a vehicle for passing wealth down the generations. To what extent is this the case? Or do many wills simply shift wealth across to people of the same generation rather than downwards? In order to answer these questions, we have grouped together types of kin beneficiary who share the same generational position in relation to the testator, where the will gives the basis for identifying this: ascendant generation (parents); the same generation (spouse, siblings, cousins); first descendent generation (children, nieces, and nephews); second descendent generation (grandchildren, great-nieces and great-nephews) and finally third descendent generation (great-grandchildren).

Certain generations are mentioned only very infrequently in wills. We have only two cases of bequests to a relative from an ascendant generation; these were both cash gifts, one to an uncle, the other to a father-in-law. Of course the uncle could be of a similar age to the testator since it is possible to have an older sibling who has a child of a similar age to oneself. However, in general the absence of beneficiaries from ascendant generations is probably a reflection of age differentials

TABLE 4.5. *Inclusion of relatives from particular generations × Type of will*

	Total estate wills		Composite wills		All wills	
	N	%	N	%	N	%
Same generation	244	59	205	53	449	56
First descendent generation	134	32	297	77	431	54
Second descendent generation	8	2	101	26	109	14
Third descendent generation	0	0	5	1	5	0.6
Ascendant generation	0	0	2	0.5	2	0.25

FIG. 4.3. Combinations of generations included in wills × Type of will

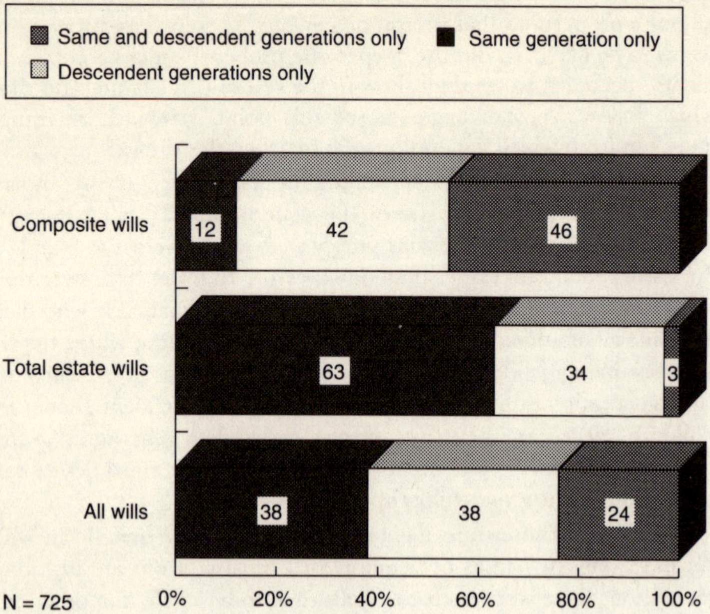

Note: these figures refer to wills which include relatives only, since it is possible to judge the generational position of a relative to a testator. We have not included beneficiaries from ascendant generations in this analysis as we only have two cases.

between generations and this implies a prediction that older generations are unlikely to survive the testator. It may also reflect normative understandings about the order in which different generations should die (Finch and Wallis, 1993). Bequests to kin in the third descendent generation are also negligible. We have only five examples and all are great-grandchildren (see table 4.5, final column). For wills written before the Perpetuities and Accumulations Act 1964, solicitors may have advised against the inclusion of great-grandchildren since such gifts might well have been invalid unless all were named individually.

A relative's generational position clearly does relate to the likelihood of the testator's naming them as a first line beneficiary, as table 4.5 shows. In generational terms, most bequests go to a relative of the same generation (56 per cent), followed closely by one from the generation immediately descendent (54 per cent). The latter is almost

FIG. 4.4. Combinations of included generations × When will written

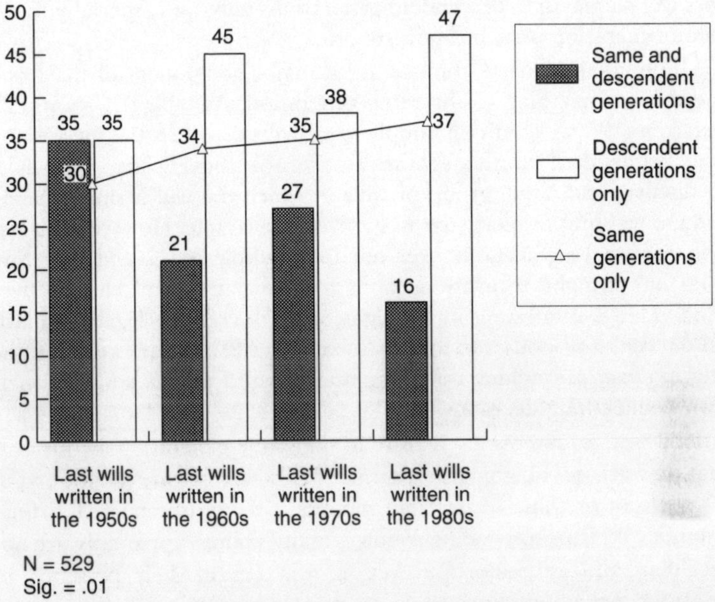

Note: the 'time' variable used here is constructed by means explained in chapter 1 and includes about two-thirds of the sample of wills.

four times more likely to appear in a will than the second descendent generation (14 per cent).

Another important feature is that testators are far more likely to bequeath exclusively to a single generation at first line, be it the same generation or a descendent generation, than they are to include beneficiaries of both same and descendent generations in the same will (see figure 4.3, bottom line). However, as we shall go on to show, generational patterns clearly vary with the value of the estate.

Figure 4.4 shows that there have been changes in these patterns over time, indicating a gradual but steady increase in the proportion of testators who bequeath exclusively to the same generation (significance .01). At the same time there has been a notable but slightly uneven decline in wills bequeathing to same plus descendent generations, though a small increase in the proportion of testators who include only descendent generations. Thus there is an apparent pattern of increasing polarisation, with a greater likelihood over time that testators will bequeath to descendent generations only, and especially to the same generation only, but not to both.[1]

Undoubtedly gifts to spouses are a major component of the trend towards bequeathing to the same generation. As table 4.1 shows, 25 per cent (196 wills) in our sample were wills in which the total estate was bequeathed to the spouse as the sole beneficiary. This is a distinctive, and large, group of wills in which the will is simply being used to transmit property to the survivor of a couple. However, this has not increased significantly over our four sample years, and therefore does not straightforwardly account for the patterns of change over time. This is interesting in the light of the increasing legal emphasis on the rights of spouses to inherit (see chapter 2) and indicates that the law, in effect, is catching up with patterns which people adopt in their own bequeathing decisions.

However, an interesting feature of the 'same generation' bequests is that they are not all going to spouses. Whilst spouses are mentioned in 37 per cent of wills, 18 per cent mention siblings (see table 4.4, final column). Whilst—as we show below—many siblings apparently are not receiving gifts of major portions of the estate, their presence in relatively large numbers suggests that bequeathing involves more than simply supporting a spouse and/or transmitting property to the next generation.

Again comparisons with previous research are difficult. The Diamond Commission found that overall wealth was split evenly between the same generation and descendent generations. However, only in the lowest-value estate did the majority of wealth go to the same generation; for all the other higher-value estates, descendent generations were bequeathed a greater percentage of the total disposable estate. Indeed in the higher-value estates there was a significant increase in the percentage of wealth left to the second descendent generation (Diamond Commission, 1977: table 87, p.176 (see table 4.4)). Our own data simply look at the presence of different generations in wills, but this too varies with the value of the estate. The estates in our three lowest quartiles are less likely to include beneficiaries from both the same and descendent generations than are estates in the highest quartile (see table 4.6).

[1] We should note that these patterns may apply particularly to our oldest group of will-makers (over 75) because of the particular measure of time we are using, in which this group is over-represented (see chapter 1).

TABLE 4.6. *Combinations of included generations × Estate value (Estate values divided into quartiles, with value 1 the lowest)*

	Estate Value 1		Estate Value 2		Estate Value 3		Estate Value 4*	
N = 625	N	%	N	%	N	%	N	%
Same generation only	61	36	85	46	73	40	59	32
Descendent generation(s) only	76	45	70	38	79	43	52	28
Same plus descendent generation(s)	33	19	30	16	32	17	75	40
Total	170	100	185	100	184	100	86	100
Sig. = .00								

**Notes*: 1 the 'same generation' category includes the small number of members of the ascendant generation. For calculation of estate values, see note to figure 4.2.
2 The 'Sig.' figure given here, and on certain other tables and figures, is an outcome of a chi-square test. As with all such tests, the meaning of this figure needs to be interpreted in the light of sample and cell size.
3 The total number of wills is 625 in this table. This represents the number of wills in which we could identify generations.

We would argue therefore that the issue of which generations are named as beneficiaries demonstrates that more complex processes are underpinning bequeathing decisions than is apparent on the surface. In order to understand this further, we need to bring into the analysis the *form* in which bequests are made. We move onto this in the next main section.

Who gets excluded?

Before leaving this initial overview of who get mentioned as beneficiaries, we can say something brief about people who do not receive gifts. For this purpose we are relying solely on the information available in the wills themselves. What we have coded is data on people who are mentioned in the will but who do not benefit from it, either at first line or as substitute beneficiaries. About one-fifth of wills excluded someone in this way (19 per cent, 155 wills).

The majority of the people who are thus 'excluded' (70 per cent) are people who have been named as executors but who are not named beneficiaries.[2] We considered their position in chapter 3 (see especially table 3.5). The remaining excluded cases, which account for only 4 per cent of all wills (27 wills), are people mentioned somewhere else in the will but who do not receive a bequest. The majority of these wills are professionally written. In a few of these cases the testator has given an explanation for why the person is not to receive a bequest. For example, one home-made will in our sample was written by a man who left his entire estate to his housekeeper and includes a comment where he makes clear his intention to prevent his estranged wife and their son from benefiting from his will:

> Nothing must go to my wife Mrs Millbank whom I have not seen for many years as I have been legally separated *By Court* and don't know her whereabouts. Also nothing must be given to my son who I have never seen since he was a baby.

However, this kind of comment is very unusual in our sample of wills. In the case cited here, it is also interesting to note that a court probably would not accept the testator's stated wishes if the estate contained ample funds to provide for both the housekeeper and the son (*Re Debenham (deceased)* (1986) 16 Fam Law 101). In general, past conflicts are rarely mentioned in wills (only 1 per cent giving any hint of them) and are also rarely explicitly presented as a reason for excluding someone (accounting for only 3 per cent of the people excluded from wills).

Nine per cent of those excluded are people who were a named beneficiary but whose gift was removed when the testators altered their will by codicil. One such example is of a woman who, in her original will, bequeathed to her niece a cash gift and a share of the residue. This testator subsequently wrote two codicils, each revoking one of the niece's bequests until finally she was no longer a beneficiary of the will. This testator did not make clear her motivation for removing the bequests to her niece. Others make it very clear why they are removing a bequest. One reason sometimes given is that the beneficiary may have received the gift or be deemed to have been sufficiently provided for during the testator's lifetime so that the

[2] Professionals who are named as executors are not included in these figures.

original bequest is removed. This was explicitly stated as the motivation behind excluding 1 per cent of the people in our sample of excluded people.

It is difficult to draw general conclusions from these data about who is likely to be excluded from a bequest because of conflict, or to lose their gift in a codicil, because the numbers are small. We are also keenly aware that there may be many 'excluded' people of whom we have no knowledge because they are not mentioned at all. However, one thing is apparent from the cases which we have identified: the individuals and the circumstances of their exclusion are highly varied. It seems likely therefore that this aspect of bequeathing operates in a very individualistic way.

Bequests: two types of will.

As we have already mentioned, previous research has been more concerned with how much of the estate beneficiaries are bequeathed than what specific types of property is left to them. However, when we look at the types of property left in our wills, some very interesting patterns are apparent.

The most striking is the distinction between wills which refer to the total estate and those which mention the residue plus other types of bequest. In our analysis we refer to the latter as 'composite' wills. In chapter 3 we discussed the legal basis for these different forms of wills and gave examples. Briefly, a 'total estate' will is one which, in its simplest form, bequeaths in the following way: 'I devise and bequeath all my real and personal estate whatsoever to my wife absolutely'. Of course not all total estate wills bequeath to a single individual. Some testators in total estate wills divide their estate between several beneficiaries (for example, their children), either giving equal shares or leaving different beneficiaries different portions of the estate. So the point about total estate wills is not that there is a single beneficiary (though this is indeed quite a common pattern); rather that the *form* in which the bequest is made is distinctive. In total estate wills no distinction is made between different types of property; all property is simply added together and then bequeathed. By contrast, composite wills specify certain types of property (including, often, sums of money) to be given to named individuals, before adding the remainder of the estate together to form the residue which then is bequeathed to one or more beneficiaries.

In just over half of our 800 wills the testators bequeath their estate as

FIG. 4.5. Whether the will was professionally written or home-made × Type of will

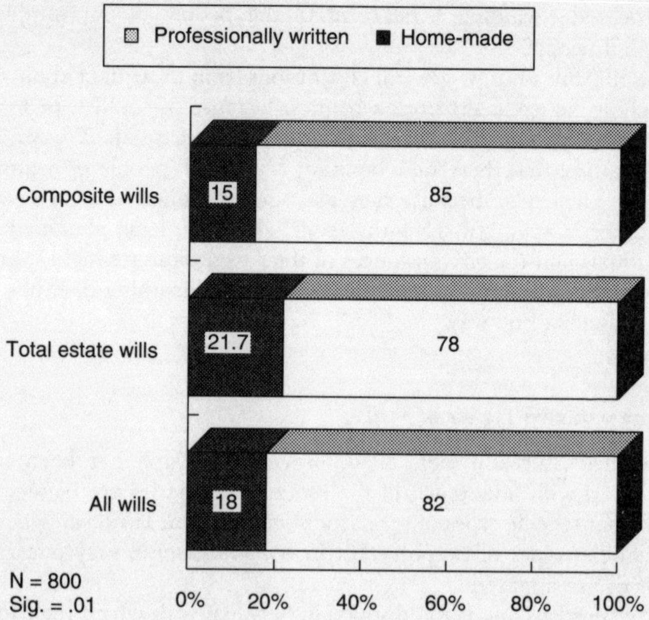

a totality (52 per cent, 414 wills). The remaining testators (48 per cent, 386 wills) break up their assets into component parts (see table 4.1, fourth section). The proportion of testators choosing to write these two types of will has not changed significantly over time. The majority of both types of will are drawn up with the assistance of professionals. However, the proportion is significantly higher for composite wills (85 per cent) than for total estate wills (78 per cent) (see figure 4.5).

The distinction between these two types of will has emerged as important in our analysis. It is not merely that they represent two different ways of bequeathing in a technical sense. They also, we have found, relate to other patterns in our data in ways which suggest two different underlying rationales, or frameworks of meaning, related to the act of bequeathing. This will emerge in the course of our analysis.

The two types of will differ from each other in certain fundamental ways, for example, in the numbers of beneficiaries named. On average, total estate wills have 1.5 beneficiaries compared with 5.6 in composite wills. Of course by definition composite wills must have at least two beneficiaries, since the testator is dividing up his or her assets in order

TABLE 4.7. *Presence/absence of close kin × Type of will written*

	Total estate		Composite estate	
	N	%	N	%
Close kin present	366	88	343	89
Close kin absent	48	12	43	11
Total	414	100	386	100
Sig. = .84				

Note: the 'absence' of close kin means simply that none are mentioned in will.

to give different items to different people. However in principle total estate wills also could be used to divide assets proportionately between a range of beneficiaries; in practice they seldom are. Seventy-seven per cent of our total estate wills bequeath to a single individual. Even where they include more than one beneficiary, 60 per cent of total estate wills mention just two beneficiaries, compared with 15 per cent of composite wills. Conversely, composite wills are far more likely than total estate wills to contain six or more beneficiaries (composite 37 per cent; total estate 10 per cent). Thus composite wills are more typically associated with a form of bequeathing which acknowledges a wide range of people in the will.

Not only do composite wills have more beneficiaries in total, but these tend to be drawn from a wider range of people. Total estate wills are much more likely than composite wills to name only kin as beneficiaries (total estate 88 per cent, composite 55 per cent) (see figure 4.1). Composite wills focus much more on transmission to

TABLE 4.8. *Presence/absence of distant kin × Type of will written*

	Total estate		Composite estate	
	N	%	N	%
Distant kin present	12	3	109	28
Distant kin absent	402	97	277	72
Total	414	100	386	100
Sig. = .00				

descendent generations than do total estate wills (see table 4.5). Spouses predominate in total estate wills, being mentioned in almost half. Indeed one quarter of our wills sample (25 per cent, 196 wills) consist of total estate wills which bequeath to the spouse alone (see table 4.1). In composite wills, children are named more frequently than spouses. Whilst total and composite wills are equally likely to include close kin (see table 4.7), total estate wills are more likely to focus on a narrower range of kin. Composite wills are more likely to include more distant kin (see table 4.8). Further, composite wills are more likely to include non-kin (see figure 4.1). Other differences between the two types of will emerge as our analysis proceeds.

What types of property are mentioned in composite wills? Some types of property are more frequently mentioned, others less frequently (see table 4.9). By far the most common is cash. Indeed one-third of composite wills simply make cash gifts and then bequeath the residue. Cash gifts range in size from £5 to £80,000.[3] The lowest cash gift for each decade in which the wills were written has not increased a great deal (from £5 in the 1950s to £25 in the 1980s). However the highest-value cash gift is twenty-five times higher in the 1980s compared with the 1950s (from £3,000 in 1959 to £80,000 in 1989). This means the range of sizes of cash gift has widened over time. As we would predict, the size of the average cash gift also increased over time. In the 1980s it was thirteen times larger than the 1950s figure (rising from £193 to £2,633). Does this larger absolute size of the average cash gift also denote that cash gifts represent a higher proportion of the average estate in wills written more recently? The answer would appear to be no. In the 1950s the average cash gift was 3.5 per cent of the average estate size; this figure only rose to 4 per cent in the 1970s.[4] So whilst the range of cash gifts has increased, other aspects of bequeathing cash gifts have remained constant. A bequest of £100 remained the most frequently mentioned cash gift in the 1950s, the 1960s, and the 1970s and only in the 1980s did it rise to £1,000.

Bequests of personal property feature in half of the composite wills. Personal property takes many forms, with general personal property being more common than a specific item such as a piece of jewellery, for example:

[3] All these figures include cash bequests to *individuals* at first line and not cash bequests to groups. Whilst we may know the size of the cash gift bequeathed to each member of a group (although this is not always clear), we often do not know the number of members. We therefore cannot calculate the average cash bequest in respect of groups.

[4] We do not include a figure for 1989 since we do not have an exact figure for the estate size for each will.

TABLE 4.9. *Types of property bequeathed at first line in composite wills*

	N	% of composite wills	% of all wills
Cash	288	75	36
Personal property	192	50	24
Houses	87	23	11
Businesses	7	2	0.9
Land	4	1	0.5
Income	13	3	1.6
Money in bank account	13	3	1.6
Non-liquid financial assets	34	9	4

I give free of all death duties to my wife Laura McClean absolutely all my personal chattels as defined in section 55(i) (x) of the Administration of Estates Act 1925 but the gift shall take effect subject to any specific effects herein contained made by any Codicil hereto.

Not all wills refer to the 1925 Act; other wills simply use the term 'general personal property' or refer to 'all household goods or items of personal effect' left by the testator in his or her home. Broadly speaking the term includes 'all articles of personal use or ornament and all the contents of home, but excludes money, securities for money, and chattels used at the death of the intestate for business purposes' (Clark, 1988: 84).

When particular items are named in wills they tend to be gifts of jewellery and specified household items, with relatively few bequests of items which are identified (or might be classified) as antiques, clothing or cars. It is quite interesting that some testators choose to bequeath household items, albeit rather a small number (5 per cent of all wills). We might expect people to name a particular ring or antique chest in their will but bequests of kitchen ware or even rugs are perhaps more surprising. Here is an example of a will which includes such items. It was written by Annie Marshall in the 1960s and includes such clauses as:

To my brother the said James Greaves my travelling alarm clock and pink carpets.
To my sister Elsie Greaves all my brassware, prestige cooker and small electric fire.
To my sister May Richards my food mixer and dressing table set.

To my step-son Henry Marshall my late husband's pocket watch and large electric fire.
To my step-daughter Susan Davison my standard lamp and electric kettle

This makes interesting reading but, as one might expect, it is relatively rare for someone to go into such detail about their personal property or indeed to bequeath such apparently mundane items of property as pink carpets and electric fires. Where a will has been professionally drafted it is likely that a solicitor would discourage the inclusion of such items, suggesting instead that they be put into a side letter if the testator wanted to give some indication of his or her wishes (see chapter 3 and Masson, 1994). The tendency to bequeath these different types of property has changed very little over time.

Other types of property, businesses, and land appear in only a few wills. Income for life and non-liquid financial assets are slightly more popular types of bequest (see table 4.9). Houses are assets which we might imagine more likely to appear in wills. However, only 11 per cent of all wills (23 per cent of composite wills) specify a house, occasionally more than one. In the majority of wills where at least one house is mentioned, the testator's house is a specified bequest (86%); but if we count the total number of houses mentioned, almost a quarter (23%) of houses being bequeathed are houses other than the testator's home. The percentage of composite wills which mention houses has not varied over the four decades in which the wills were written. This does seem surprising, given the rapidly increasing rates of home ownership between 1959 and 1989, a phenomenon which provided one of the starting-points for this study (see chapter 1). The fact that it is still quite rare to find houses mentioned specifically in probated wills is probably attributable to a combination of three factors. First, it may simply be too soon for significant changes in home ownership to be reflected in probated wills, since many 'new' home owners will still be alive (Hamnett and Mullins, 1992). Second, houses have increasingly been owned jointly between married couples, and would therefore pass outside the will (see chapter 2). Third, the apparent emphasis on a surviving spouse simply receiving all (or most of) the estate—a factor which we discuss elsewhere in this analysis—is likely to lead to bequests to spouses in a form which does not differentiate houses from other types of property. We conclude therefore that a house forms an increasingly important part of a spouse's inheritance, but often it will not be specified in the will (either because it is already owned jointly or because it passes as part of the total

FIG. 4.6. Patterns of estate value × Type of will

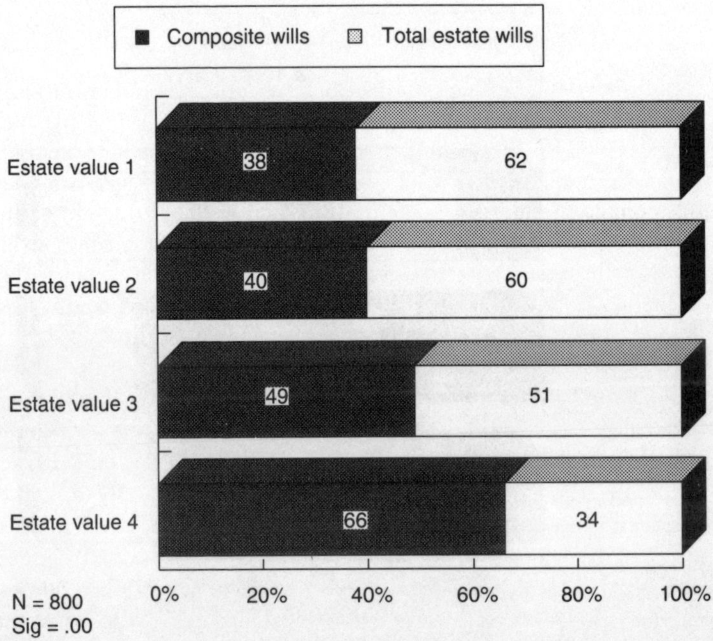

Note: for calculation of estate values, see note to figure 4.2.

estate). It is only in the will of the surviving spouse her or himself that we may find more houses specified in the future, as increased rates of home ownership work their way through to the inheritance received by the next generation. Indeed this point is emphasised by comparison between patterns of bequeathing of married and widowed women. Sixteen per cent of widows bequeath a house explicitly compared with 10 per cent (7 wills) of married women.

Who leaves their estate in the form of a composite will, and who opts for the total estate formula? Are there any common characteristics of testators which can be identified in our two different types of will? One factor is certainly estate size. There is a distinct relationship between the two types of wills and estate values. People who have estates of high value are more likely to specify particular assets in their wills (see figure 4.6). This may make sense simply because possessing more assets gives more scope for division.

Another interesting difference between total estate and composite

Fig 4.7. Gap between date of will and testator's death × Type of will

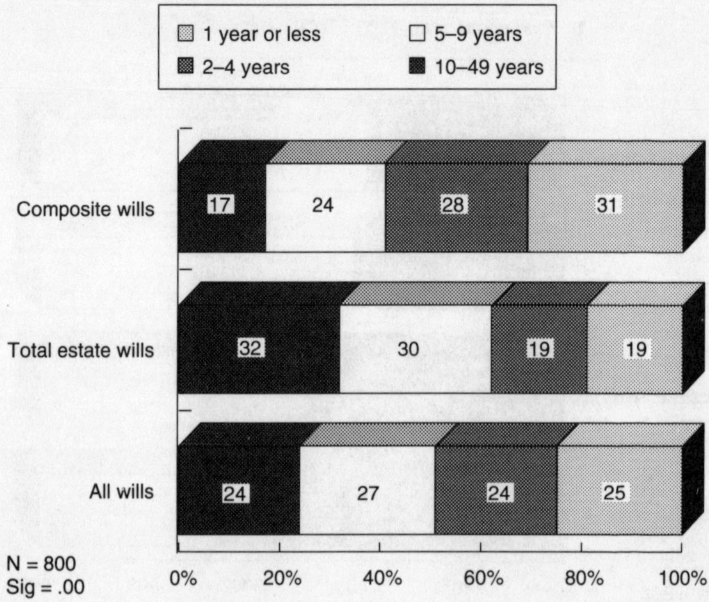

wills concerns the date when the will was written. As we indicated in chapter 3, one-quarter of the wills were more than ten years old at the time of the testator's death; the rest were more up-to-date, with the median gap being just under five years. When we divide the wills into total estate and composite, we find some interesting patterns (see figure 4.7). It appears that more total estate wills had been written well in advance of death, with 62 per cent more than five years old and 32 per cent more than ten years old. The comparable figures for composite wills are 41 per cent and 17 per cent. Conversely composite wills (31 per cent) are more likely than total estate wills (19 per cent) to have been written within a year of the testator's death. Since there is a tendency for people with larger estates to have more up-to-date wills, this may be a factor in the relationship between types of will and estate size (figure 4.6); however this relationship is not statistically significant.

Alongside this we need to look at another factor, namely the testator's age. Older testators are more likely than younger ones to write composite wills and this is particularly true for the over 75s, who are almost three times more likely than those under 60 to write

TABLE 4.10. *The inclusion of distant kin in the will × Age of testator*

	60 and under		61–75		Over 75	
	N	%	N	%	N	%
Distant kin present	5	4	46	14.5	61	24
Distant kin absent	139	97	271	85.5	198	76
Total	144	100	317	100	259	100
Sig. = .00						

TABLE 4.11. *Inclusion of close kin in the will × Age of testator*

	60 and under		61–75		Over 75	
	N	%	N	%	N	%
Close kin present	133	92	283	89	221	85
Close kin absent	11	8	34	11	38	15
Total	144	100	317	100	259	100
Sig. = .09						

composite wills (figure 4.8) This links with our finding that testators aged over 75 are six times more likely than those aged 60 and under to include in their wills the more distant kin groups such as in-laws, step-relatives or blood relatives such as great-grandchildren, great-nieces, great-nephews or cousins (see table 4.10), although this pattern is not repeated in the presence of close kin groups (see table 4.11). Older testators are using a variety of gifts to acknowledge a range of beneficiaries which would appear to suggest will-making has a very different meaning for the older and the relatively younger will-maker.

From a legal perspective total estate wills are more appropriate for younger testators since gifts are likely to be eroded by changes in the testator's circumstances or by inflation, and all manner of things can happen to items of personal property between drafting the will and death. However, we would argue that this age pattern reflects more than professional understandings of appropriate will-writing. Let us

FIG. 4.8. Type of will × Age of Testator and whether the will is home-made

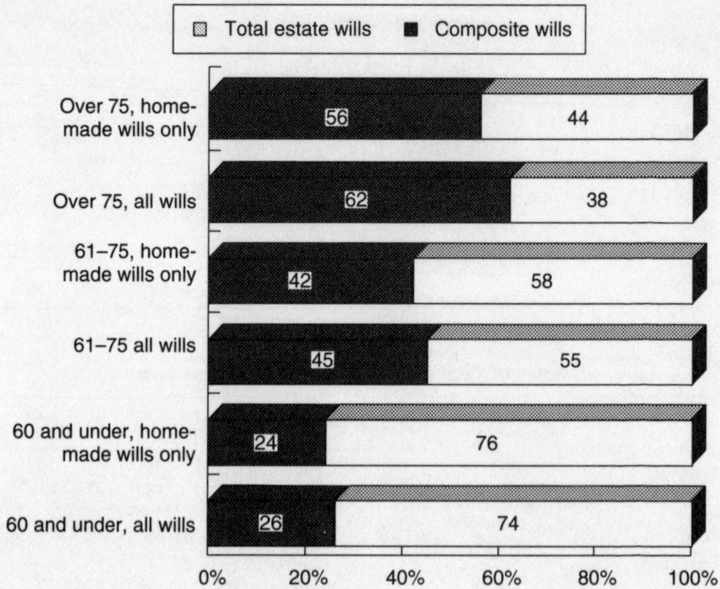

N = 720 (all wills), 130 (home-made wills)

focus on those wills which were not professionally made which are more likely to be total estate wills than those written by professionals.[5] For testators aged 60 and under, 76 per cent of the home-made wills were total estate yet for testators aged over 75 the figure falls to 44 per cent (see figure 4.8). The decrease by testator age in use of total estate wills, even amongst elderly testators who choose to write a home-made will, does not support the hypothesis that age differences in the type of will written can be explained by the influence of professional advice.

It would seem therefore that the use of the different types of will by older and younger testators has a meaning other than simply being an artefact of the will-making process. We have argued elsewhere (Finch and Wallis, 1993) that wills written by younger people may simply be seen as safety nets to provide for circumstances which the testators do not believe will really occur in the near future, namely their own death. For elderly people, particularly the over 75's, the closer reality of death

[5] 60 per cent of home-made wills are total estate compared with 50 per cent of professionally written wills. See also Fig. 4.5.

FIG. 4.9. Marital status and gender of the testator × Type of will

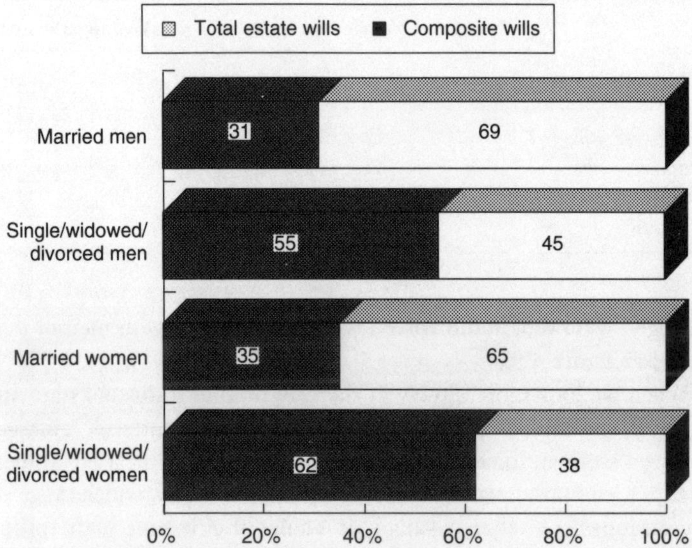

N = 364 (men), 389 (women)

apparently leads more of them to go into more precise detail about what they wish to happen to their assets (Finch and Wallis, 1993). The older the testator—and the closer they are to death when they write their last will—the more likely is it that the will takes a composite form, acknowledging a range of personal relationships with a specific gift.

The other type of testator characteristic linked with the two types of will is marital status, which itself is linked to gender. Testators who are not married at the time of writing the last will are more likely to write composite wills than are those who write their last will in the context of an extant marriage. As we have already noted (chapter 3), women will-makers are less likely to be married at the time of writing the will than are men (though of course they may well have been married previously). Thus we find that, although there is no clear gender difference across the sample as a whole on this issue, when we add together gender and marital status we find some interesting patterns. A higher (though not statistically significant) percentage of married women write composite wills, compared with married men. This pattern is repeated

TABLE 4.12. *Marital status of women × Type of will*

	Married women		Widowed women	
	N	%	N	%
Total estate wills	47	65	46	31
Composite wills	25	35	104	69
Total	72	100	150	100
Sig. = .00				

for single, widowed, and divorced women compared with men of that status (see figure 4.9).

When we look more closely at the way marital status links in with the way women bequeath, further interesting patterns emerge. Widowed women, for example, are twice as likely as married women to write a composite will in which they acknowledge a wider range of relationships (see table 4.12). This could also be the pattern for widowers when compared with married men. Unfortunately we cannot explore this as widowers are seldom identified as such in wills. However, the justification for concentrating on the actions of widows rests upon women's greater longevity. For the majority of couples in Britain, it is likely to be the widow rather than the widower who makes the final decision about the disposal of the couple's assets (Finch and Hayes, 1995).

In the process of exploring the different testator characteristics associated with total estate and composite wills[6], we can therefore begin to see that the differences are more than technical. It would seem that the act of bequeathing, through the mechanism of a will, means different things to different testators. Composite wills offer an opportunity for a range of relationships to be acknowledged with specific gifts, and in that sense are more personal and individualistic. It would seem that the opportunity to bequeath in this way is one taken up by the relatively wealthy, by those who are older and or closer to death when they write their will, and by people (more likely to be

[6] We have not mentioned regional differences here, though we allowed for a regional comparison in the construction of our analysis. In relation to the difference between total estate and composite wills we found no indication of regional variations. As this is true throughout our analysis we have not pursued the regional dimension.

FIG. 4.10 The probability that a testator will write a composite will (Z) for different groups defined by age, marital status, gender, and estate value

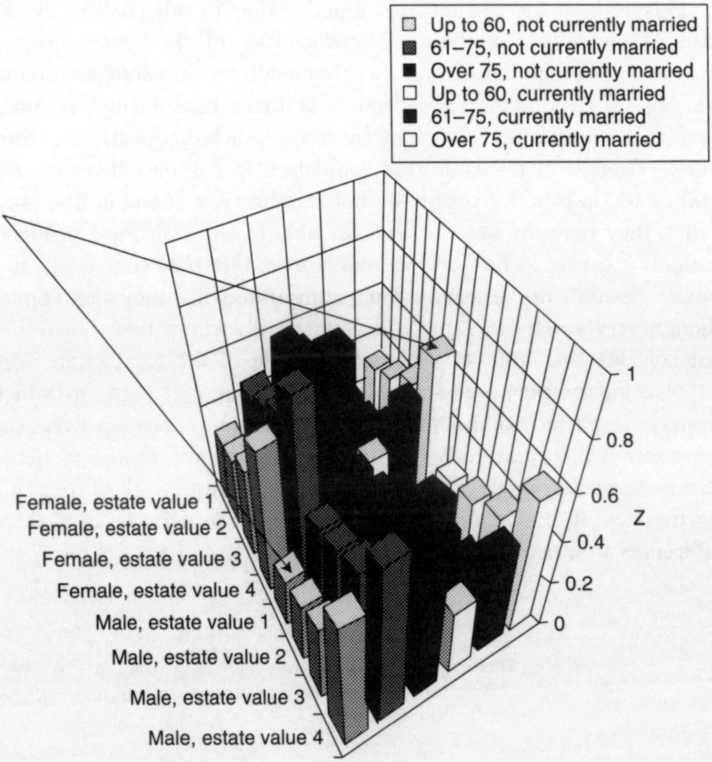

Note: for calculation of estate values, see note to figure 4.2. The highest figure for Z is .86057, the lowest is .09622.

women) who are not married at the time when the will is written. Indeed this is confirmed when we look at the probability that a testator in our sample will write a composite will. It is the unmarried female, aged over 75, with an estate from the highest band (Value 4) who is most likely to write a composite will. Least likely to write such a will is the married male, aged 60 or less with an estate from the lowest band (Value 1). This is illustrated in figure 4.10, which has been produced from a multiple regression analysis to explore the relationship between a number of variables. Here we are examining how combinations of testator characteristics (age, gender, marital status, and the value of the estate) relate to the way in which testators divide their estate.

This adds to the picture, developed earlier in this chapter on the basis of our initial analysis of beneficiaries, of the quite complex processes which are involved when bequeathing decisions are made. We can now see that the reflection of those complexities is much clearer in composite wills than in those which bequeath the total estate. Though in principle one could have a complex division of a total estate, in practice people do not use this type of will in that way; rather, they typically use this as a formula to transmit their property straightforwardly to one or two individuals. Often of course this is a spouse. Spouses do appear in some composite wills; they also appear (though very rarely) in some total estate wills where there are other beneficiaries (see table 4.1). But the vehicle of the total estate will, bequeathing simply to the spouse, is the dominant form in which property is passed to the survivor of a couple. Those who use the composite will format—whether or not they include spouse as beneficiary—seem to be operating with a different framework of meaning for the act of bequeathing. The following chapters explore these differences in more detail.

5 Who Gets What? Principles of Bequeathing

In this chapter we put together the 'who' and the 'what' in wills, to explore further the principles at work when people make their bequeathing choices at first line. We also look at conditions which are placed upon bequests in certain wills. In exploring the principles of bequeathing by these means, we are keenly aware that we should be cautious about attributing particular types of motivation to will-makers. Working simply from wills, one has only limited access to the reasons why testators might have made particular bequeathing decisions. We do believe however, as we argued in chapter 1, that the patterns observed across the whole data set can be used to understand what outcomes testators in general hope to produce through the formal legal mechanisms available to them. It is in this sense that we explore the 'principles' of bequeathing in this chapter.

Who gets what?

In the previous chapter we noted that, unsurprisingly, spouses and children figure prominently in wills and that, beyond them, most beneficiaries are drawn from a restricted range of kin (siblings, nieces, nephews, grandchildren). We can now take this further by linking the identity of the beneficiary with the type of gift each is likely to receive. In doing this we are posing two sets of interrelated questions:

1. Are there characteristic types of gift associated with different categories of kin? Or do bequests given vary more individually according to circumstance?
2. What generational, genealogical, and consanguineal patterns underpin bequests which different kin types receive?

In our own data there are two ways of approaching these issues, using different units or levels of analysis: the will or the individual beneficiary. We can explore these questions at the will level by asking, for example: of those testators who include a gift to a child, how many are giving that child a house? The second approach looks at the questions from the perspective of the beneficiary, for example: taking all the children mentioned in the wills, what types of gift are children most likely to receive? Each approach complements the other. However, in interpreting the data it must be borne in mind that it was the wills which were randomly sampled; the beneficiaries themselves are not necessarily a representative sample. For instance, we could have sampled one will which has a large number of gifts to nieces or nephews which may then distort the data on what is bequeathed to that particular group of beneficiaries. In the following analysis, therefore, we refer to patterns which emerge from both sets of data: data on how testators bequeath and on what individual beneficiaries are likely to receive.

We begin by exploring the impact of generation on what is bequeathed. There are two ways in which we can tackle this. First, we can treat generation as a single variable, adding together all beneficiaries in the same generation as the testator (spouse, sibling, cousin), all in the first descendent generation (child, niece, nephew), and so on. This produces some quite interesting patterns, but we can understand them better if we tackle generation in the second way, as separate variables related to different lines of descent. This means that we look at generational relationships in the testator's own direct line of descent (spouse, child, grandchild) and compare them with the parallel line of descent for the testator's sibling (sibling, niece/nephew, great-niece/nephew). Our analysis follows through these two ways of handling the variable of generation.

Using generation as a single variable, a notable feature is that there is a difference between the two types of will, as we noted in chapter 4. Total estate wills overwhelmingly feature exclusive bequests to a generation, most usually to the same generation as the testator. Twenty-five per cent are accounted for by an exclusive bequest to a spouse. By contrast, composite wills characteristically include more bequests to descendent generations and are most likely to combine them with a bequest to the same generation (see figure 4.3). Thus the pattern of bequeathing in composite wills is more variable in generational terms.

What more can we learn if we look in more detail at the specific gifts which beneficiaries in different generations receive, breaking down composite wills into their main component parts? Figure 5.1 shows the different generational patterns for the three most common types of gift which appear in wills (total estate, residue, cash). The most popular gift to relatives of the same generation is a share of the total estate; for one generation descendent, a share of the residue; and for

FIG. 5.1. Most popular types of gifts bequeathed × Generational position of first choice beneficiaries (relative to testator)

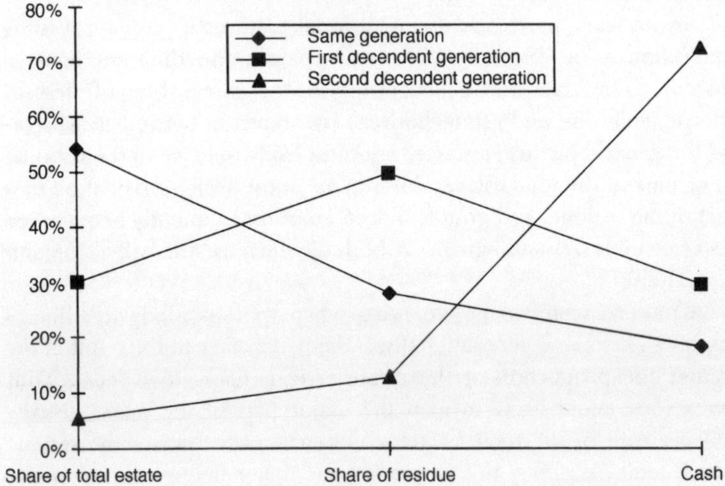

N = 725

Note: this figure looks at generational position of kin, using only those beneficiaries for whom we can make fairly accurate guesses about their generational position vis-à-vis the testator. Like all the figures in this chapter, it uses the will as the unit of analysis.

two generations descendent, cash. This suggests that testators are not substituting beneficiaries in the desdendent generations for 'missing' ones in the same generation, giving, for example, to a child or grandchild what they would have left to a spouse. Rather, this pattern suggests that people think about the appropriate bequests for each generation in qualitatively different terms.

A further pattern emerges if one considers the likely value of these gifts received in practice. Whereas the value of gifts of total estate or residue will depend on the testator's economic circumstances at the time of his or her death, cash gifts are fixed at an absolute level at the time when the will is written. Thus people in the same and first descendent generations typically get 'variable' gifts (in this sense), whilst bequests to people in the second descendent generation are 'fixed'. The *relative* value of variable and fixed gifts may be anticipated by the testator at the time of writing the will, but of course their relative values may have changed by the time that the estate is divided. From the wills themselves we have no way of knowing how far testators might consider the unpredictability of relative values at the time of writing a will.

Can we learn more about generational patterns if, instead of using generation as a single variable, we separate the different lines of descent? The data for beneficiaries in the direct line of descent (spouse, children, and grandchildren) are shown in figure 5.2. Mirroring the general picture, testators are most likely to leave to their spouse all or part of the total estate, children are most likely to be left all or a part of the residue, and grandchildren are most frequently bequeathed cash (see table 5.1 and figure 5.2, both of which use the will as the unit of analysis).

A pattern seems to be emerging when we look along this line of descent. The closer, generationally, is the beneficiary to the testator, the greater the proportion of the estate s/he is likely to receive. Thus spouses are more likely to gain the major part of the estate (usually 100 per cent of the total estate), children tend to receive the residue (which tends, but may not always be, the major bequest in composite wills), and grandchildren are more likely to receive small bequests of cash.

Is the same pattern repeated in gifts to different generations in the sibling's line of descent? Figure 5.3 shows that the generational distinctions in this line of descent are different. Siblings (30 per cent) are twice as likely as niece/nephews (15 per cent) to be left a portion of the total estate. To that extent the position of siblings is similar to that of spouses, their counterparts as same generation beneficiaries in the direct line of descent. However, the analogy breaks down when we compare it with figure 5.2. Siblings are equally likely to be given a share of the residue or cash. The same applies to niece/nephews. So there is not the same sense within this particular line of descent, especially in relation to the gifts of residue and cash, which are found in composite wills, that certain types of gift are appropriate for different generations.

This analysis of generational patterns suggests that generational position plays an important role in shaping both who gets a bequest and the type of bequest received. However, the comparison of different lines of descent indicates that genealogical position (relative to the testator) also affects who gets what. To explore the point about genealogy further, we can add to our analysis some information on gifts received by more distant kin. Drawing on table 5.1, we can see that cash is clearly seen as the most appropriate type of bequest for more distant kin and for non-kin. Seventy-one per cent of cousins, 63

TABLE 5.1. *Analysis of types to property bequeathed to different beneficiary types*

	Total Estate		Residue		Cash		Testator's Home		Personal Property	
	N	%	N	%	N	%	N	%	N	%
Spouse N = 294	199	68	66	22	10	3	25	9	25	9
Child N = 291	107	37	147	51	41	14	34	12	38	13
Grandchild N = 93	5	5	10	11	66	71	4	4	4	4
Great-grandchild N = 7	0	0	1	14	5	71	0	0	0	0
Sibling N = 146	43	30	50	34	48	33	9	6	21	14
Niece/Nephew N = 137	21	15	65	47	67	49	9	7	14	10
Great-Niece/Nephew N = 19	1	5	4	21	13	68	0	0	0	0
Sibling-in-law N = 41	3	7	10	24	26	63	2	5	4	10
Step-Child N = 13	2	15	5	39	5	39	1	8	0	0
Cousin N = 17	2	12	7	41	12	71	0	0	3	18
Friend N = 60	7	12	10	17	46	77	3	5	6	10

Note: this table uses the will as the unit of analysis. Each percentage is calculated on the number for its own row. In some cases the total for the row is more than 100% because, to take the example of siblings, (i) there may be more than one sibling in the will with different siblings receiving different gifts and (ii) a single sibling may receive more than one type of gift.

FIG. 5.2. Most popular types of gift bequeathed to first choice beneficiaries in the direct line of descent from the testator

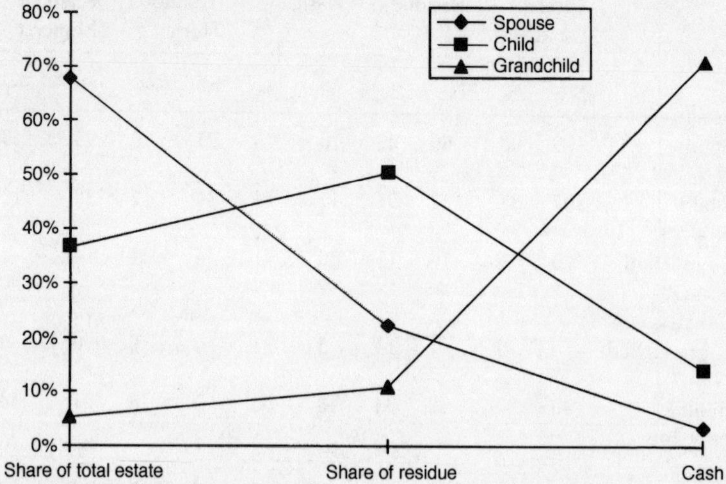

N = 531

Note: this figure used the will as the unit of analysis.

per cent of siblings-in-law, and 77 per cent of friends who receive a bequest get a cash gift. However, if we take the case of step-children, patterns of bequeathing are less clear. Step-children are as likely to receive a portion of the residue as they are to receive cash. This suggests that they are not being treated in the same way as blood children who more frequently are bequeathed a share in the residue. However, neither do they predominantly get cash bequests like distant kin.

When we pull together the strands of analysis related to generation and genealogy, it seems that for close kin on the one hand, and more distant kin plus non-kin on the other, the 'appropriate' type of bequest is very clear. Kin within the direct line of descent are very likely to receive a gift which varies according to their generational position. Distant kin, affines, and non-kin are likely to receive a cash gift. Therefore a model starts to emerge which could be conceptualized as concentric circles, where the type of gift deemed most appropriate to both the inner and outer circles is fairly predictable. However, in the 'intermediate' circle, in terms of closeness to the testator, patterns are less predictable. In this 'intermediate circle' we find step-children, nieces, nephews, and siblings. What these kin are likely to receive is

FIG. 5.3. Most popular types of gifts bequeathed to beneficiaries in the testator's siblings' line of descent

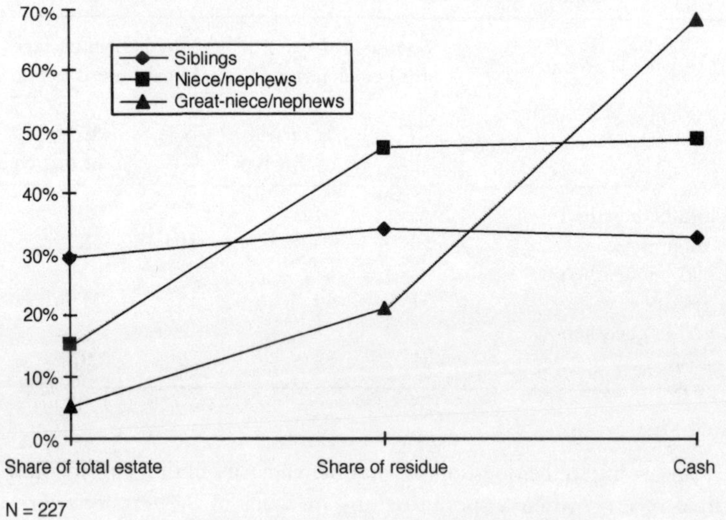

Note: this figure uses the will as the unit of analysis.

much more variable, perhaps based on a more individualistic appraisal of relationships with particular people (an issue to which we return later in this chapter).

However, before leaving this issue we need to consider another possible explanation of the patterns in our data. Could it be that the gifts received by kin in the 'intermediate' circle are affected by whether there are close kin mentioned in the will? Do kin in the group which we have called 'intermediate' get used as 'replacements' for close kin if, for example, a testator has no surviving spouse or children?

If we look generally at whether the presence of certain beneficiaries influences what others are likely to get, it is evident that the presence of a spouse has a significant impact, especially in total estate wills. In these cases, when a spouse is present in a will, children are far less likely to receive bequests of total estate (5 per cent, 3 cases) than when spouse are absent (46 per cent, 104 cases) (see table 5.2). Yet interestingly in composite wills the presence or absence of a spouse does not seem to affect the likelihood that children are bequeathed part of the residue. Again, different logics of bequeathing appear to be at work in these two different types of will.

TABLE 5.2. *The type of bequest bequeathed to child × Presence or absence of testator's spouse in the will*

	Spouse and child are beneficiaries		Child is beneficiary but spouse is not	
	N	% of wills of this type	N	% of wills of this type
Child bequeathed total estate	3	5	104	46
Child bequeathed residue	31	49	116	51
Child bequeathed cash	21	33	20	9

Returning to the question of what beneficiaries in the 'intermediate' circle receive, when a spouse or any member of the testator's direct blood line is present in the will, both siblings (63 per cent, 20 cases) and niece/nephews (72 per cent, 16 cases) are more likely to be bequeathed cash. When the direct line of descent is not mentioned, both siblings (40 per cent, 46 cases) and niece/nephews (53 per cent, 61 cases) are more likely to be left a share of the residue. In these latter cases, it looks as if the sibling, niece or nephew is acting as a replacement beneficiary for someone genealogically closer, in situations where testators are without close kin (or possibly, where they have decided not to bequeath to their close kin). What constitutes the underlying principles of such 'replacements' is an issue to which we shall return in chapter 6, where we analyse the use of substitute clauses linked to the possibility that a first choice beneficiary will die before the testator.

A slightly different way of looking at this idea of replacements is to ask: do testators appear to have a clear concept of a 'next of kin', a beneficiary who is treated similarly whatever their genealogical relationship? Or do the patterns of bequests related to kin type, which we have identified above, appear to override any concept of a 'next of kin'? Of course we cannot know what ideas people have in their minds when they are writing wills. But we can make a comparison between those wills which contain a spouse and/or children and those where the genealogically closest kin are siblings, nieces or nephews. We find that 69 per cent of wills which mention a spouse or child (whom we

FIG. 5.4. The relationship between the beneficiaries' status as 'next of kin' and the portion of the estate which they receive

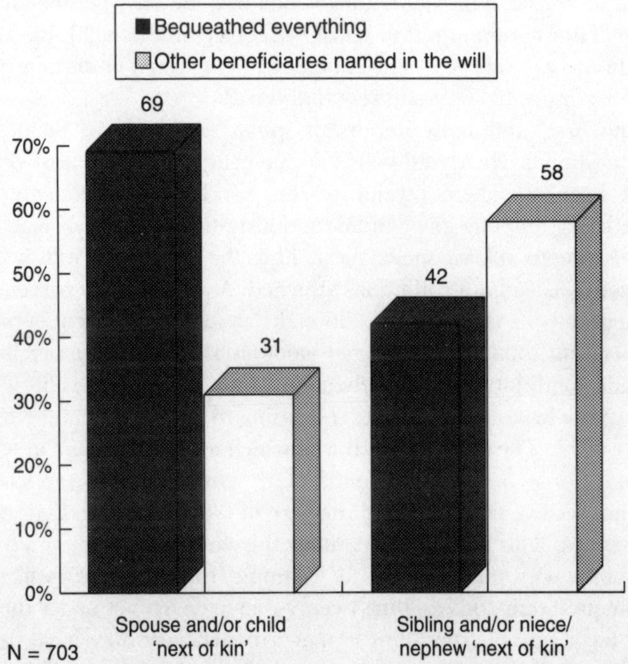

Note: this figure uses the will as the unit of analysis.

would take to be the testator's 'next of kin') bequeath everything to them; the remaining 31 per cent mention another beneficiary alongside the spouse and/or child(ren). Only 42 per cent of wills in which siblings and niece/nephews appear to be the next of kin (that is, where neither spouse, child nor grandchild appears) bequeath everything to the sibling and the niece/nephew. Thus being in an apparent 'next of kin' position does not, of itself, constitute a factor which completely overrides genealogy and generation in determining the gift which a particular individual is most likely to receive.

We therefore have identified three factors which seem to interlock to form underlying principles of bequeathing: genealogical position, generational position, and being 'next of kin'. These interact in complex ways, as we have shown, and also take different forms in total estate and composite wills.

On what terms are bequests made?

We now consider the conditions which may be set when bequests are made. How common is it to make bequests conditional? What kinds of conditions are set? Are certain types of beneficiary, or certain types of bequest, more likely to attract conditions?

The first, and most important, point is that most bequests are unconditional. Nearly all wills (97 per cent) include at least one outright bequest, where receipt of the gift is not dependent on the beneficiary fulfilling any condition. Thirty-five per cent of wills attach a condition to at least one bequest. Thus the majority of wills bequeath *all* their gifts without conditions attached. A much higher percentage of composite wills include a conditional bequest (42 per cent composite, 29 per cent total estate). Higher-value estates are also more likely to include conditional bequests than wills with lower estate values (29 per cent of the lowest-value estates increasing to 45 per cent in the highest-estate wills). The types of conditions which testators include in wills are varied. Some beneficiaries, particularly children and grandchildren, will not receive their gift until they are of a specified age. Eighteen per cent of the wills (142 cases) contain this condition. Sometimes age is combined with marriage, so, for example, the beneficiary will receive the bequest only 'on reaching twenty-one or marrying under that age'.

A less common condition is that a beneficiary may have use of a bequest until they marry (0.9 per cent, occurring in 7 wills). This is associated with giving rights to occupy the testator's home until the beneficiary marries, when (presumably) it is deemed s/he will no longer need the home. One female testator allows a man (whose identity is unclear) to remain in her house, making the following conditions:

> No sale of my dwelling house 20 Drovers' Lane Romford aforesaid shall take place during such time as John Priestly continues to reside therein provided that he is residing at my address at the date of my death and that he shall be entitled to have the use and occupation of the property and be responsible for the repairs and all outgoings including General and Water Rates and insurance Subject to him remaining unmarried.

If John were to marry the house would then became part of the residuary estate and be divided between nephews.

The other six wills in which there are conditions relating to marriage (or more particularly, remarriage) are all written by men. All but one involve giving an income to a wife until she remarries, and three apply such a condition on the bequest of a house. An example is the following, taken from the will of a testator who died in 1959:

I give to my trustees of this my will such effects of household or domestic use of ornament as my said wife shall within three months after my death select upon trust to permit my wife to have the use and enjoyment thereof during her widowhood she keeping the same in good repair and conditions (reasonable wear and tear excepted) and insured to full amount thereof against fire and so that after her death or remarriage (which ever shall first occur) the same shall fall into and form part of my residuary estate. . . . I give to my wife as from my death and so long as she remains my widow an annuity of seventy eight pounds.

There is something of a common theme in wills which attach conditions to bequests of houses or household property. It concerns the testator's wish to ensure that a spouse, cohabitee or other relative retains the right to the house previously shared, but only whilst s/he continues to live within the context of the relationship which that shared home represents.[1]

A similar rationale may lie behind the use of another type of condition, namely life interest. In these cases, the beneficiary enjoys the use of the bequest for his or her lifetime, but thereafter it passes to other beneficiaries who have been specified by the testator. Ultimately then the 'liferent' (the beneficiary who receives the bequest for life) is not free to dispose of the property as s/he wishes, as would be the case with an outright bequest.

Seven per cent (56) of our wills involve the creation of a trust for part or the whole of the estate. Most of these are cases where the testator's spouse is the liferent and the property reverts to the testator's children on the spouse's death. There is an association between the bequest of a house and the creation of such a trust. Whilst only 5 per cent of bequests of general personal property are settled for life on the beneficiaries, some 33.3 per cent of houses are so limited. Given that it is rare for testators to mention houses specifically in the will, it is interesting that, when houses are specified, one-third of testators do not give the house as an outright gift.

Three per cent of wills include a gift of income-generating property. The source of the capital for these trusts varies. In four wills the trust was created from the testator's entire property, in fourteen wills from

[1] The implications of passing on a shared house are discussed more fully in Finch and Hayes (1994).

the residue. Very uncommonly we find trusts created from a fixed sum of money (2 cases) or the cash from the sale of a house (2 cases). If we look a little more closely at this subset of wills it is interesting to note that almost half have the highest-value estate size and three-quarters were written pre-1968 when there would have been tax advantages to be gained from setting up such trusts. As with the condition of remarriage there appears to be a link between the inclusion of life-time-only gifts and the gender of the testator. Male testators are almost twice as likely as female to include this condition, whilst married testators are three times more likely than unmarried testators to bequeath a gift for the beneficiary's life only. So whilst (as we outlined in chapter 4) married people and perhaps more commonly, married men, are more likely to write the simpler total estate wills, we see also that they are more likely to make bequests of gifts for a beneficiary's lifetime only or include conditions of remarriage in their will.

We have commented so far on the position of spouses in particular and noted that, where a conditional bequest is made involving a spouse, it is likely to be associated with the use of the former marital home. However, in general, conditions are less likely to be attached to bequests to spouses than they are to those involving other beneficiaries. As we move down the generations from spouse to grandchild, on the surface the pattern seems to be that the further the beneficiary from the testator in generational terms, the more likely is s/he to have a condition attached to the bequest, with grandchildren quite consistently receiving the lowest number of unconditional bequests. However, most of the conditions attached to descendent generations are related to the age at which the gift will take effect. If we remove age-related conditions from the analysis, there is no significant relationship between the generation of the beneficiary and the likelihood that a condition will be attached to the bequest.

These then are the main patterns which can be derived from the minority of cases where conditions are attached to bequests. Beyond these, our wills contain an eclectic range of instructions which do not fall within any of the above patterns and which we have recorded as 'other' conditions. Some of these would be legally binding, others not. They range from stipulating how a beneficiary should spend his or her cash gift, to directing executors that a cash gift may be paid only if the estate is above a certain value thus turning a 'fixed' bequest into a semi-'variable' one. Some wills attach some very specific and unique conditions to a gift which were clearly introduced to meet the changing circumstances in which the testator finds herself or himself. An example of this is to be found in the will of Amy Dixon, a woman from South East England. It is clear that between her first will and subsequent codicil Amy's care needs changed and this had implications for the provisions she made for her beneficiaries. In her first will, written in 1986, the testator appeared to be living in her own home which she bequeaths, along with the land which surrounds it, to her grandson. Two years later, Amy wrote a codicil from an address which appeared to be a nursing home. In the codicil she changes the terms of this gift to her grandson, requiring him to contribute to the cost of her own care as a condition of accepting the gift:

> Now I hereby revoke the said gift and I give the said property Lodge Farm House and the surrounding land . . . to my grandson Matthew Freeman absolutely subject to any mortgage charge or any other liability subsisting thereon at my death and subject to and charged with the payment by Matthew Freeman to my daughter Pamela Brown of such of the sums as amounts to one half of all Nursing Home Rest Home or Private Hospital or medical fees paid or payable by me or my Estate from the 1st of May 1988 until the date of my death and Matthew Freeman in accepting the gift of Lodge Farm House shall be personally liable for such payment to Pamela Brown.

There are various possible reasons for these conditions, on which one can speculate. But really the most notable feature, from the perspective of the will sample as a whole, is how few attempt to tailor the bequest to the specific conditions of the beneficiary's life, a feature which may be influenced to some extent by solicitors (Masson, 1994). For the most part, the writers of wills seem to be content to make bequests unconditional, and this is particularly true of testators writing home-made wills. Whilst professionally written wills are as likely as home-made wills to include an unconditional bequest they are also twice as likely to include a gift with a condition attached. As many as 86 per cent of home-made wills attach no condition to any bequest in the will compared to 60 per cent of wills written with professional advice (see figure 5.5). It may be that people who wish to make complex wills are more likely to seek professional advice than those who do not. We should also note that lawyers' concerns about home-made wills, on the grounds that testators may use complex formulations and thereby unintentionally create trusts (see chapter 3), may be misplaced or at least exaggerated. Where conditions are set, they are most likely to occur in composite wills, again reinforcing the impression

FIG. 5.5. The presence of conditional and unconditional bequests in a will × Who drew up the will

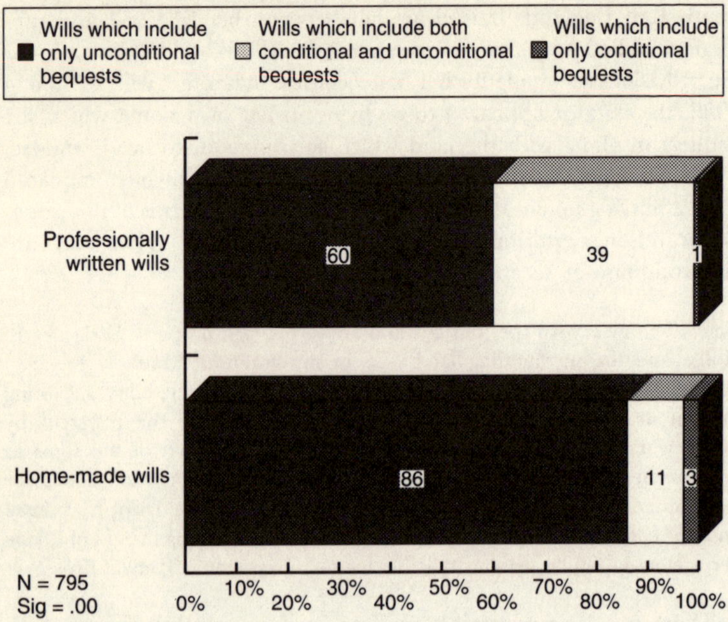

Note: Five wills are excluded from this analysis because they bequeath to charities and other organisations. They were therefore not coded in the 'individual beneficiaries' file, from which this analysis is drawn. This figure uses the will as the unit of analysis.

that the framework of meaning associated with these is different from total estate wills.

Differential treatment: the circumstances and characteristics of beneficiaries

In our discussion of conditions attached to bequests we have begun to see that the life circumstances of the testator may, in some cases, affect the way in which a bequest is made or the type of gift received. We consider now whether there are any more general ways in which bequests seem to be affected by the life circumstances or personal characteristics of the beneficiary. For example, does being married appear to influence what children receive, by comparison with unmarried children? Does this operate differently for sons and daughters? Questions like this explore whether there is differential treatment of beneficiaries within a kin type (in this example, linked to marital status and gender). Looking for patterns across the wills sample as a whole, we are trying to work out whether patterns of bequeathing are linked in any systematic ways to the life circumstances or personal characteristics of beneficiaries. Alternatively, it may be that being a grandchild or cousin of the testator is the overriding factor influencing bequests, and that therefore personal circumstances are irrelevant. We concentrate here on looking for systematic differences across the wills sample as a whole; in the next section we will explore whether distinctions are made in a more individualistic way, comparing the treatment of different beneficiaries within a single will.

We begin with the issue of gender, and consider how far this seems to influence the pattern of bequests, within each kin type. Table 5.3 gives data on this issue, based on what is received by different types of kin and using the individual beneficiary as the unit of analysis. Its basic message is that gender is not particularly important. Certainly gender differences within a kin type appear to have much less relevance to the type of bequest received than does membership of a particular kin category. For example, the likelihood of receiving a portion of the residue is slightly greater for sons (55 per cent) than it is for daughters (51 per cent); but both sons and daughters are far more likely than are beneficiaries of any other kin type to receive this particular type of bequest. The same holds true, in broad terms, for other kin types.

However, if we look at gender differences across all kin types, a slightly different picture emerges. The small gender differences within each kin type, when put together, look like more of a pattern. In composite wills women receive more bequests 'overall' of the testator's home and general personal property. Men meanwhile are a little more likely to be bequeathed the residue than are their female counterparts. However, whilst the testator's home is a more popular gift for females, the amount they receive is often smaller. Therefore in composite wills we do get some sense of there being 'women's bequests' and 'men's bequests', a phenomenon which would have been very familiar in the past as historical studies show (Davidoff and Hall, 1987). However, in our wills sample this seems to operate at the margins and in a minority of cases, rather than driving the distribution of property in a more central way. It indicates that the rationales which, in the past, apparently led to different treatment of male and female beneficiaries are now much more muted.

In total estate wills there are also some gender differences. Females of any kin type are consistently more likely to receive bequests of total

TABLE 5.3. *A comparison of what is bequeathed at first line to male and female individuals of the same kin type*

	Total Estate		Residue		Cash		Testator's Home	
	N (% of this kin type)	Mean % of gift received	N (% of this kin type)	Mean % of gift received	N (% of this kin type)	Mean £ amount of gift received	N (% of this kin type)	Mean % of gift received
Wife N = 226	156 (59)	100	49 (18)	93	9 (3)	1853	19 (7)	97
Husband N = 68	43 (63)	98	17 (25)	96	2 (3)	200	6 (9)	100
Daughter N = 271	89 (33)	61	138 (51)	46	31 (12)	1884	24 (9)	63
Son N = 279	87 (31)	51	152 (55)	44	33 (12)	5352	20 (7)	80
Grand-daughter N = 68	1 (2)	20	6 (9)	23	51 (75)	569	3 (4)	33
Grandson N = 279	2 (2)	38	11 (12)	39	69 (76)	893	2 (2)	75

Sister	35	75	47	55	48	1172	10	75
N = 160	(22)		(29)		(30)		(6)	
Brother	11	61	23	44	30	616	1	100
N = 77	(14)		(30)		(39)		(1)	
Nieces	33	37	70	39	89	1110	3	100
N = 204	(16)		(34)		(44)		(2)	
Nephews	19	42	61	39	81	557	6	67
N = 173	(11)		(35)		(47)		(4)	
Cousin (F)	0	0	0	0	18	373	0	0
N = 22	(0)		(0)		(82)		(0)	
Cousin (M)	(0)		(0)		5	300	(0)	
N = 22	(0)		(0)		(39)		(0)	
Friend (F)	0	0	0	0	75	276	0	0
N = 95	(0)		(0)		(79)		(0)	
Friend (M)	0	0	0	0	27	498	00	0
N = 33	(0)		(0)		(82)		(0)	

Note: this table uses the individual beneficiary as the unit of analysis.

estate than are their male counterparts. Also, with the exception of grandchildren, nieces, and nephews, the amount of total estate women receive, on average, is a higher percentage than that received by men of the same kin type. Thus, for example, daughters receive on average 61 per cent of the total estate and sons 51 per cent; sisters receive 75 per cent and brothers 61 per cent (see table 5.3). So in total estate wills female beneficiaries tend to be favoured, in the sense that they are likely to be receiving a higher proportion of the estate than their male counterparts, taking our wills sample as a whole. If anything, in composite wills this pattern is reversed. We thus conclude that, whilst there are some gender differences in patterns of gifts received, the direction of these differences is not consistent. Moreover, such differences as do occur are less important than kin type in determining the type of bequest received.

Equally, it would appear that the marital status of the beneficiary does not have a notable or a consistent effect on the bequests received. In order to explore if there is any relationship here, we will concentrate on the contrast between what is bequeathed to daughters, sisters, and nieces of differing marital status. The data for this are given in table 5.4 (again, using the individual beneficiary as the unit of analysis). Since the numbers are rather small in each cell it is difficult to discern patterns. Nevertheless, spinster daughters and siblings seem more likely than their married counterparts to receive a bequest of a house or share of it. Similarly, a larger proportion of spinster siblings and nieces receive a share of the total estate compared with their married counterparts, although this is not the case for children where, as we have indicated before, the issue of treating equally seems to be more important.

The other feature of beneficiaries' circumstances which we are able to explore, and which might have an impact, is the geographical proximity of the beneficiary to the testator. The majority of testators include the addresses of beneficiaries in their wills. From this information it has been possible to code the proximity of each beneficiary to the testator and to explore whether this bears any relationship to what the beneficiary is bequeathed. We consider here whether kin who live closer to the testator have a greater chance of: (a) receiving major bequests (total estate, residue) more frequently, or (b) being given a larger share of a particular gift. We will concentrate on three kin groups: children, siblings, and niece/nephews. Our comparison simply uses two categories of geographical proximity, comparing what is

TABLE 5.4. *Type and amount of bequest × Marital status of beneficiary*

	Total Estate		Residue		Cash		Testator's Home	
	N (% of this kin type)	Mean % of this type of gift	N (% of this kin type)	Mean % of this type of gift	N (% of this kin type)	Mean £ amount of this type of gift	N (% of this kin type	Mean % of this type of gift
Spinster Daughter	5	53	8	58	3	108	3	67
N = 24	(21)		(33)		(13)		(13)	
Married Daughter	51	54	69	47	15	904	10	63
N = 189	(27)		(37)		(8)		(5)	
Spinster Sister	12	71	9	35	5	614	4	75
N = 31	(39)		(29)		(16)		(13)	
Married Sister	10	64	16	43	17	1451	4	75
N =54	(19)		(30)		(32)		(7)	
Spinster Niece	4	17	1	20	5	172	0	0
N = 12	(33)		(8)		(42)		(0)	
Married Niece	4	40	16	52	13	543	0	0
N = 37	(11)		(43)		(35)		(0)	

Note: this table uses the individual beneficiary as the unit of analysis.

left to kin who share a home, or live in the same street or town, with kin who live further away.

For children at least, proximity does appear to have some bearing on what is bequeathed (see table 5.5), though the effects are not dramatic. Children who live near to their parents are more likely to receive the testator's home or receive bequests of total estate (the less common bequest for this kin type) than children living at a distance from their parents; however this pattern does not hold for gifts of the residue. There also appears to be differential treatment in terms of *how much* is bequeathed to children who live close to and at a distance from their parents. With the exception of cash gifts those children living closer appear on average to be bequeathed a larger share; but again the average difference in the shares bequeathed is not large except in the case of shares of the testator's home.

Proximity appears to have a particularly important association with bequests to siblings. Following the same pattern as for children, siblings near to home are bequeathed more, and bigger, shares of the range of gifts analysed except cash gifts. This suggests an intuitively understandable difference in the level of commitment to a sibling who lives within closer proximity to the testator, and a willingness to tailor the type of gift to the circumstances of a particular relationship, in ways which do not quite apply to niece/nephews. In the case of niece/nephews the association between proximity and the bequest is not repeated.

It would seem therefore that, of the beneficiary characteristics which we have been able to explore, geographical proximity is the only one which is likely to make some difference to patterns of bequeathing, though our conclusion here must be tentative since it is based on the analysis of individual beneficiary data which (for reasons explained above) are not necessarily a representative sample. Even in relation to proximity, the likely impact varies for different kin types. Neither gender nor marital status would appear to have any consistent or predictable effect. Of course there may well be other beneficiary characteristics (for example, economic circumstances) which do have an effect, but one which cannot be accessed through the data contained in wills. We can, however, get some sense of whether this kind of individual circumstance is likely to be taken into account by looking at the types of variation which occur within a single will.

TABLE 5.5. *Type of bequest bequeathed to kin groups × Geographical proximity (where known)*

	Total Estate		Residue		Cash		Testator's Home	
	N (% of this kin type)	Mean % of gift received	N (% of this kin type)	Mean % of gift received	N (% of this kin type)	Mean £ amount of gift received	N (% of this kin type)	Mean % of gift received
Children Live close N = 90	32 (35)	59	43 (48)	60	10 (11)	1245	9 (10)	85
Children Live at distance N = 95	28 (30)	57	54 (57)	44	9 (10)	1855	6 (6)	47
Siblings Live close N = 51	16 (31)	82	22 (43)	69	8 (16)	772	7 (14)	71
Siblings Live at distance N = 66	12 (18)	58	21 (32)	49	29 (44)	1812	3 (5)	83
Niece/Nephews Live close N = 37	5 (14)	70	17 (46)	60	15 (41)	383	0 (0)	0
Niece/Nephews Live at distance N = 136	23 (17)	30	53 (39)	36	62 (46)	1040	6 (4)	75

Note: this table uses the individual beneficiary as the unit of analysis.

Differential treatment: individual variations

The second type of 'differential treatment' which we consider reaches to the heart of the questions which we are exploring in this study. It pinpoints the issue of how far bequeathing decisions are concerned with recognizing and honouring individual relationships, rather than simply being driven by the underlying principles which we have already identified (genealogical position, generational position, being 'next of kin'). We do this by focusing on the following questions. Within a single will, do people of the same kin type always receive the same and/or equal gifts? If not, which groups are most likely to receive differential treatment? What is the nature of this differential treatment?

In fact nearly a quarter of our wills (22 per cent) treat people from the same kin type differently, and the rest treat them on identical terms. This indicates that a significant minority of will-makers do think in individual terms when deciding on bequests. However, many of these cases of differential treatment, on an individual basis, probably do not represent gifts of significantly different economic value. For example 18 per cent of our wills bequeath different types of gift to beneficiaries of the same kin type. However, this often entails leaving each different member of a kin category a different item of personal property: one is bequeathed an item of jewellery whilst another receives a piece of furniture, for example. Such cases of differential treatment often appear to reflect gendered understandings about what constitutes an appropriate gift for a male as opposed to a female beneficiary so that, for example, a male testator may give his own watch to a son whilst a daughter receives a clock, more obviously a domestic item than a piece of 'male' personal property. In certain cases the different types of bequest may represent gifts of different economic value, for example where one niece receives a cash gift whilst other niece/nephews are left shares of the residue. In general, this large group of 'differential treatment' cases, where beneficiaries in an equivalent genealogical position receive a different type of gift, represent circumstances in which a clear distinction needs to be made between the symbolic and material value of gifts. It is evident that objects which are bequeathed specifically and individually embody a symbolic meaning which reflects the value which the testator places on his or her relationship with the beneficiary. In that sense, such gifts are highly personal even though there are some systematic patterns related to gender in particular. However, in terms of economic value, insofar as one can judge this from the information given in wills, these gifts typically appear to be roughly equivalent to each other within the context of a single will.

Turning to other forms of differential treatment, a much lower percentage of wills (5 per cent) divides a particular bequest unequally between beneficiaries of the same kin type, for example giving different portions of the residue to different individuals. This is a form of bequeathing which appears not only differential but also economically inequitable from the beneficiary's standpoint. However, we cannot know from the wills data whether it would be experienced as inequitable, nor indeed whether it might be a strictly equitable bequest perhaps compensating for another gift during the testator's lifetime by evening out the balance. In any event, probably the most important point to note is that, whilst this type of differential treatment certainly does occur, it is comparatively rare.

Other forms of differential treatment are even less common. Three per cent of the wills accord beneficiaries of the same kin type different beneficiary status; that is, some are first line beneficiaries whilst others only receive bequests as substitutes. (We deal with the issue of substitution in chapter 6). Finally, we have coded wills which exclude a member of a kin type from benefiting from the wills (1 per cent of our wills) whilst others benefit under varying conditions. Both of these types of will do appear to vary the value of the bequest within kin type, as of course do bequests which give varying portions of the same gift. However, in general, our conclusion must be that differential treatment normally entails acknowledging the individuality of specific relationships, whilst maintaining the principle that people of the same kin type are treated broadly on equal terms.

Are any types of beneficiary particularly likely or unlikely to attract differential treatment? The relevant data are given in figure 5.6, which uses the will as the unit of analysis. The numbers here are small because the analysis is confined to those wills which do include some form of differential. From these data it appears that niece/nephews and cousins are the kin types most likely to receive differential rather than equal treatment. At first glance there appears to be something of a pattern: the further is the beneficiary genealogically from the testator the more likely is s/he to attract differential treatment.

However it is also apparent, as with other aspects of bequeathing,

FIG. 5.6. The equal and differential treatment received by different kin types, in wills which include differential treatment

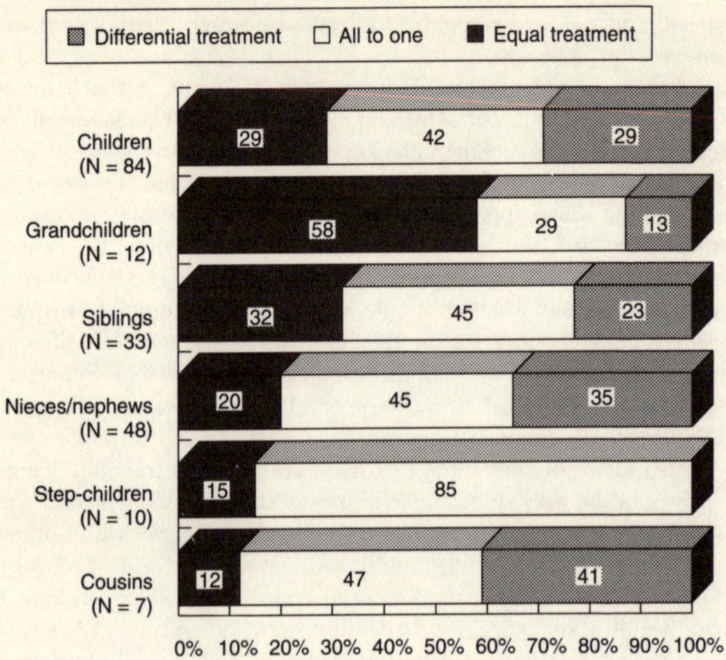

Note: this figure uses the will as the unit of analysis.

that generational position is important as well as genealogy. If we exclude from the analysis those cases where only one person of a particular kin type is mentioned in the will, we see that grandchildren are the group least likely to receive differential treatment. This reflects the fact that grandchildren are the beneficiaries most likely to receive a group bequest which does, by its very nature, bequeath members of the group the same type and amount of a gift. The same pattern occurs with the small number of great-niece/nephews included in the wills, that is, with the group in the same generational position but in a different line of descent. These two groups are the beneficiaries most distant from the testator in generational terms, and a common-sense explanation would seem to be that the testator is less likely to have relationships with individuals in these groups which are both close and variable, in ways which might lead to different gifts being bequeathed. Niece/nephews and cousins, meanwhile, are generationally closer and therefore more likely to have been known personally as adults. In these cases there would also seem to be less pressure for equal treatment, perhaps because of genealogical distance. Certainly testators seem to feel freer to differentiate between one cousin and another, than between one grandchild and another.

Children and siblings represent intermediate groups here, being treated differentially and equally in roughly the same numbers. These are groups where individuals would be known intimately by the testator, and where the individuality of relationships may therefore be acknowledged by different bequests; on the other hand there would seem also to be an impulse towards equal treatment. We can understand more of this by looking at the types of differential treatment received by different groups of beneficiaries (table 5.6, which also uses the will as the unit of analysis). Where children are treated differently, it is normally the case that this means receiving different types of bequest. Often, as we have indicated, this means different personal items which seem to be roughly equivalent in value. Conversely it is quite rare for children to be given unequal shares of the same gift. Siblings however, and even more so niece/nephews, are more likely than children or indeed grandchildren to receive different shares of the same gift.

We would argue therefore that there are two different principles at work in bequeathing decisions, in relation to the differential treatment of individuals. One principle is that people in equivalent positions should receive gifts of equal value. This applies very clearly to beneficiaries in the direct line of descent, less clearly to other kin types. Children and grandchildren predominantly receive gifts of equal value. Treating people on equal terms would seem to be important for these categories of beneficiary. However, despite this, children may receive gifts partly in the form of a specific bequest which acknowledges the individuality of the relationship with the parent. This points to the other principle at work, namely that it can be appropriate in bequeathing to acknowledge individual relationships, not simply to give to people according to their kin type. Though not all testators do this in the will, where it happens it is most likely to occur with genealogically more distant kin. For these groups it may involve bequeathing gifts which are not only different in kind, but also of different economic value. With siblings, niece/nephews and other categories of beneficiary, there does not seem to be the same imperative to treat people on equal terms, though of course many testators do bequeath in that way.

We have looked at beneficiary characteristics in some detail, but is

TABLE 5.6. *Types of differential treatment received by kin types (as a % of those wills which include differential treatment for that kin type*

	Different types of bequest		Unequal shares		Different beneficiary status		Some of kin type excluded	
	N	%	N	%	N	%	N	%
Children N = 84	70	83	12	14	9	11	4	5
Grand-children N = 12	8	67	1	8	2	17	1	8
Sibling N = 33	22	67	8	24	7	21	3	9
Nieces/nephews N = 48	35	73	20	42	7	15	1	2
Great-nieces/nephews N = 1	0	0	1	100	1	100	0	0
Affines N = 10	8	80	1	10	1	10	1	10
Cousins N = 7	5	71	3	43	0	0	0	0

Note: this table uses the will as the unit of analysis. Because different bequests and unequal shares may be combined in the same will, the figures in a line may add up to more than 100%.

differential treatment also linked to testator characteristics? The most crucial factor here is the marital status of the testator and the size of the estate.[2] Testators who were not married at the time of writing their last will are three times more likely than unmarried testators to leave different gifts to people within the same kin type. This reinforces further the pattern which we noted in chapter 4, namely that widows (and other unmarried testators) appear to bequeath in distinctive ways, being more likely to acknowledge a range of relationships and—as we can now see—to do so in ways which are more likely to be personal

[2] Here a multiple regression analysis was conducted to explore the relationship between a number of testator characteristics (age, gender, marital status, and the values of the estate) and the inclusion of unequal treatment in a will

FIG 5.7. Differential treatment of beneficiaries (in wills which include differential treatment) × Time period in which the will was written

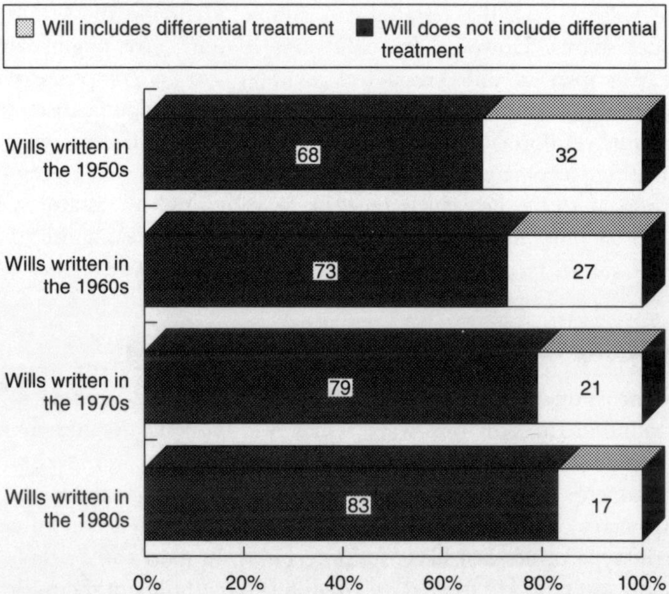

N = 179
Sig. = .01

and individual. There is an apparent link between differential treatment and estate size, with wills in the highest quartile being more likely than those in the lower quartiles to make use of differential treatment. Thirty-three per cent of wills in the highest quartile (estate value 4) make use of differential treatment, compared to 23 per cent with estate value 3 and 17 per cent with estate values 1 and 2. However, as we noted in chapter 4, estate size itself is linked to the difference between total estate and composite wills.

Perhaps of more interest are changes over time. There has been a consistent decline in the proportion of wills which use differential treatment over our four sample years. Thirty-two per cent of wills written in the 1950s contained examples of differential treatment; by the 1980s this had decreased to 17 per cent (see figure 5.7) . This change may be related to factors noted in chapter 4, especially the decline in gifts of personal property over time.

Finally, patterns of differential treatment vary in our two types of will. Though obviously composite wills give more scope for it, it is quite possible for certain forms of differential treatment to occur in total estate wills, where the testator can choose to divide the estate in unequal shares. However, in reality this is quite rare. Significantly more examples of differential treatment appear in composite wills (total estate, 5 per cent; composite, 41 per cent; significance .00). Again this reinforces the sense that there are two different types of bequeathing associated with the two types of will, and that composite wills appear to be the vehicle most likely to be used by testators who wish to include in their bequest elements which distinguish their beneficiaries in terms of relationship, not just by kin type.

Concluding remarks: principles of bequeathing

Our discussion of the principles of bequeathing has identified some important features of our wills, which we will take further in the chapters which follow. To summarise the main points, we have found that the factor of 'kin type' (that is, the precise genealogical position of a beneficiary relative to the testator) is of prime importance in influencing the type of bequest likely to be received. In most cases people of the same kin type are treated on equal terms, certainly in the sense of receiving gifts of roughly equal economic value. This is especially true of bequests to children and grandchildren, less so of those to more distant kin where it is a little more likely that individuals within the same kin type will be treated on different terms. Normally the principle of equal treatment appears to override considerations based on the personal circumstances of the beneficiary, though we have found that geographical proximity between testator and beneficiary may make some difference to the type or amount of the gift received.

In trying to understand the ways in which testators distinguish between one kin type and another when deciding upon the appropriate type of bequest, we have identified three factors: genealogical position, generational position, and whether the beneficiary occupies the position of 'next of kin'. We have argued that these three interlock in quite complex ways but that, once one understands how they operate, one can identify with considerable accuracy the type of gift likely to be received by each.

For the most part therefore bequests do come as a result of the 'positions' which people occupy within a kin network, not as a result of the specific relationship between testator and beneficiary. However, there are certain cases where there is a much stronger sense of acknowledging the individuality of relationships. This occurs in a variety of ways: setting conditions on a bequest to suit life circumstances of a particular beneficiary; bequeathing different specific items to different individuals of the same kin type; giving different individuals gifts of different value (clearest in cases where people receive differing proportions of the same gift). About a quarter of our testators thus include some element of individuality in their will, but most of them do it by bequeathing different specific items to named beneficiaries, in ways which appear not to breach the general principle of equal treatment.

Finally, we should note that composite wills are much more likely than total estate wills to contain elements of differential treatment, or to attach conditions to bequests. Indeed, in the light of the analysis in this chapter, composite wills look more clearly like a vehicle for testators to include elements in their will which are more personal and more individualistic, whilst total estate wills are very likely to treat beneficiaries simply in terms of 'positions' rather than as individuals who are distinguished one from another.

6 Patterns of Substitution

Introduction

In the previous two chapters we considered patterns of bequeathing which were based on testators' first choice of beneficiaries. However, some wills also include substitution clauses which specify what is to happen to a particular bequest in the event that a first choice beneficiary predeceases the testator. In this chapter we discuss patterns of bequeathing in these cases where entitlement to a bequest is conditional on the prior death of another beneficiary.

In examining the use of substitution we are interested not only in the patterns of bequeathing at this level in the will, but also in their relationship to the patterns which we noted at first line. When we put the two together we get the fullest picture available from wills about testators' concepts of 'family' in the context of bequeathing. We see not only who is treated as having the first claim but also the models of progression which operate as one person's claim is replaced by another's. We will also maintain the distinction, developed in chapters 4 and 5, between total estate and composite wills. We will explore how far, and in what ways, this distinction is carried on down the inheritance line.

Analysing patterns of bequeathing at substitution represents a further departure from previous research based on wills. As we noted in chapter 4, much of the work to date on inheritance has concentrated on the transmission of wealth and has used the concept of the main beneficiary to examine inheritance outcomes (Hamnett, Harmer, and Williams, 1991). A consequence is that other types of beneficiary, including those who inherit at substitution, are excluded from the analysis. However, our data show that this results in a number of beneficiaries being ignored, or their importance in the total picture of inheritance being under-estimated. Beneficiaries thus overlooked include those who enter the will only as substitutes, or those who inherit gifts of greater value as substitutes than they do as first choice beneficiaries.

Table 6.1 gives some basic data on patterns of substitution in our wills sample and we shall refer to it throughout this chapter. We shall comment briefly on its main features before moving on to discuss each

TABLE 6.1. *Patterns of substitution*

All wills (N = 800)	N	As a % of all wills	As a % of wills with substitution
i. Does the will make any provision for substitution?			
At least one substitution clause	497	62	—
No substitution clauses	303	38	—
ii. Does substitution cover all bequests made at first line?			
Substitution for all bequests	275	34	55
Substitution only for some bequests	222	28	45
No substitution	303	38	—
iii. Does substitution cover all beneficiaries named at first line?			
Substitution for all beneficiaries	300	37	60
Substitution only for some beneficiaries	197	25	40
No substitution	303	38	—
iv. Changes at substitution			
New bequests introduced	55	7	11
New beneficiaries introduced	372	47	75
Original gift divided between more beneficiaries	270	34	54

Total estate wills (N = 414)	N	As a % of all wills	As a % of total estate wills
Substitutes provided for all bequests/beneficiaries	250	31	60
Substitutes provided for only some bequests/beneficiaries	3	0.4	1
No substitution	161	20	39
Of those wills which provide full substitution (N = 250)			
—Remain total estate wills at substitution	213	27	51
—Become composite wills at substitution	37	5	9

TABLE 6.1. *Patterns of substitution* (Cont.)

Composite wills (N = 386)	N	As a % of all wills	As a % of composite wills
Substitutes provided for all bequests	27	3	7
Substitutes provided for only some bequests	217	27	56
Substitutes provided for all beneficiaries	50	6	13
Substitutes provided for only some beneficiaries	194	24	50
No substitution	142	18	37
Use of different levels of substitution (N = 497)	N	As a % of all wills	As a % of wills with substitution clauses
One level of substitution (i.e. one predecease clause)	263	33	52
At least one example in the will of two levels of substitution (i.e. two predecease clauses)	169	21	34
At least one example in the will of three or more levels of substitution	65	8	13

Note: in this table, the figures for 'bequests' and 'beneficiaries' do not match each other. This is because a given beneficiary may receive two or more bequests, only one of which is covered by a substitution clause.

in detail. In total, 497 (62 per cent) of our wills include at least one substitute beneficiary and 372 (47 per cent) introduce beneficiaries who are new to the will at this level. In addition, for a substantial number of wills, both the content of the will and the division of bequests take on different characteristics at substitution. Most commonly, there is only one level of substitution in the will (that is, one predecease clause for a given bequest), but a minority of testators include multiple levels by anticipating a series of possible predeceases.

Both total estate and composite wills use substitution in roughly equal proportions (61 per cent of total estate wills and 63 per cent of composite wills make some use of substitution). However, there is a difference in the comprehensiveness of the coverage. Whereas 60 per cent of total estate wills provide substitutes for all bequests and beneficiaries, in composite wills only 7 per cent provide substitutes for all bequests and 13 per cent do so for all beneficiaries. So in composite wills it is much more common that certain gifts will be left without a substitute, whilst others will be covered. In practice, gifts thus omitted would fall into the residue and thus the residuary beneficiaries are, in effect, the substitutes for these items.

One third of the wills (270, 34 per cent) divide gifts differently at substitution so, for example, a gift which went to a single beneficiary at first line is shared between several beneficiaries at substitution. Only 55 wills (7 per cent) use substitution to introduce new gifts to the will. The following, taken from a will written by a married male testator, is an example. The testator leaves his entire estate to his wife at first line but, should she predecease him, he determines that it should be divided in the following way. Items of jewellery, 'the former property of my wife aforesaid', are bequeathed to his granddaughter, and 'all items of gentleman's jewellery' go to his son. The sum of £5,000 is given to his daughter-in-law, with the same amount bequeathed to each of four named grandchildren, on attaining the age of eighteen years. The residue of the estate goes to his son absolutely. In this example, gifts which did not appear at first line do so at substitution (jewellery, cash gifts); new beneficiaries also appear (son, daughter-in-law, grandchildren); and the will changes from being a total estate will at first line to a composite will at substitution.

From the perspective of our particular interest in inheritance therefore, substitution clauses are very much part of the will and we need to include them in any discussion of bequeathing behaviour. Of course, we are unable to tell from the data available to us which beneficiaries actually receive their bequests in practice. In studying the content of substitution clauses, as elsewhere in this analysis, we are not concerned with predicting or analysing outcomes of inheritance. Rather, our interest in the use of substitution clauses in wills rests on what they tell us about patterns of bequeathing behaviour and the concepts which underpin it. Our point here is that an analysis of substitution clauses offers a more rounded picture of testators' bequeathing behaviour than one gets from looking at first choice bequests alone.

Substitution: the legal context

Substitution clauses thus feature in the majority of the wills in our sample. The reasons why a testator might include substitution clauses can be broadly divided into those which are personal to the testator and those which are a result of technical considerations related to inheritance law. In practice these are unlikely to operate independently, but it is important to understand the legal context within which decisions about substitution may be made.

From the perspective of inheritance law the most important reason for including substitution clauses is to prevent the possibility of a gift's lapsing or failing, and hence to prevent partial (and, in some cases, full) intestacy. Subject to an important exception which is discussed below, if a beneficiary dies before the testator, and if the will makes no provision for what is to happen in that event, the doctrine of lapse takes effect (Clark, 1988: 336). Under this rule the gift is deemed to have failed and it reverts into the residue. If the gift in question is the residue itself, then the testator is deemed to have died intestate for that part of the will. Partial intestacy is subject to the same rules as apply to full intestacy, and those individuals who would have benefited from the estate had the testator been wholly intestate take the lapsed share of the residue.

How aware of these issues is the average testator likely to be when writing a will, and how well informed about the consequences? We cannot be sure of this from wills alone, though we discussed earlier some evidence which suggests that professional advisers pay particular attention to predeceases when advising clients (see chapters 2 and 3). The wills themselves also give an indication that the input of professional advisers may be particularly significant when it comes to substitution. Seventy-one per cent of professionally written wills in our sample make some provision for substitution, whereas only 25 per cent of home-made wills do so (see figure 6.1).

However, there is also evidence from the wills sample that the introduction of substitutes is not simply a technical matter which lawyers introduce merely to ensure that their clients' wills contain no loopholes. Substantial numbers of wills, whether drawn up professionally or not, provide only *partial* substitution, that is, certain gifts are not covered by predecease clauses. This occurs in 40 per cent of wills which are professionally written and which include substitution, and in 35 per cent of home-made wills (see figure 6.2). We discuss partial substitution

FIG. 6.1. Use of substitution clauses in professionally written and home-made wills

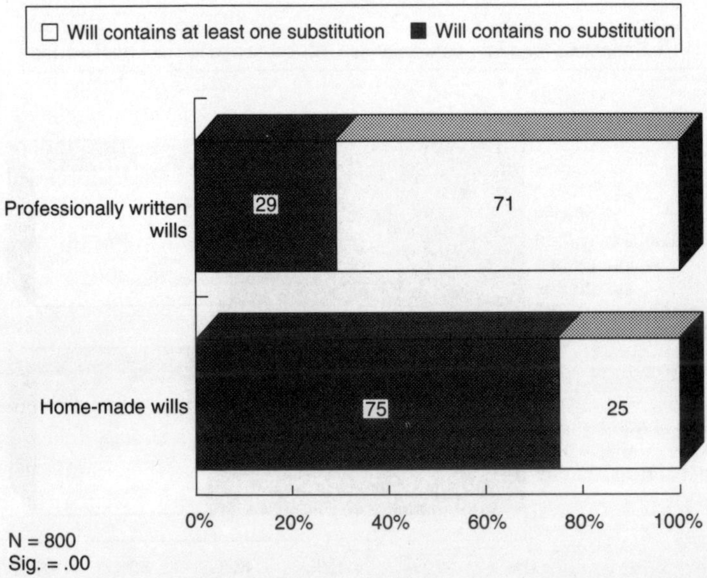

in more detail later in this chapter. Our main point here is that there seems to be evidence that both solicitors and testators are making a distinction between one gift and another, not simply treating the provision of substitutes as a technical matter.

Further, our evidence is that many wills, including many professionally written wills, contain examples of substitution which are strictly unnecessary in legal terms. This relates to a particular exception to the rule of lapse, which we need to explain before presenting the relevant data.

Bequests made to the testator's child(ren) or remoter issue are not subject to lapse. Although this has been the case since 1837, recent amendments to the law have brought about important changes which affect the outcome (Clark, 1988: 341–3). Section 33 of the Wills Act 1837 prevented a gift to the testator's issue from failing but did not ensure that it passed to the issue's successors. Under section 33 if the testator's child predeceased the testator, the gift passed into that child's estate and was distributed according to his or her will or, if no will

FIG. 6.2. Use of full and partial substitution in professionally written and home-made wills (for wills which include substitutes)

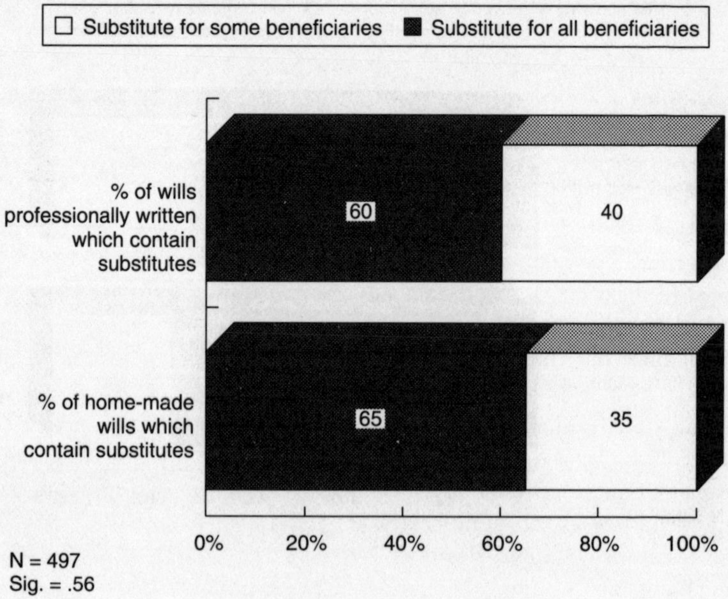

existed, the gift went to those entitled to benefit under intestacy. In some instances this could mean that the gift passed outside the testator's blood line. For example, if the child had left a spouse then s/he would stand to benefit from the gift. The spouse would then be free to dispose of the gift as s/he wished and the testator's grand-children might not benefit at all. If the surviving spouse were to remarry and produce further children, these children might ultimately benefit from the original estate, to the detriment of the testator's own issue.

Section 19 of the Administration of Justice Act 1982 brought in important amendments which effectively change that. Under the *per stirpes* rule, any gift to the testator's child or remoter issue who has predeceased the testator passes on automatically to the *issue* of that beneficiary as if s/he had been named as a substitute beneficiary. Thus the amendment ensures that a gift remains within, and passes down, the testator's blood line. These changes apply to testators who died after 31 December 1982. Thus before that date if a testator willed a gift to his or her child (or other issue) it was essential also to include a substitution clause to ensure that the gift passed down to the successor of that beneficiary in the event of the child or issue predeceasing the testator. From January 1983 onwards it is only necessary to name substitutes for gifts to friends or other relatives, or if the testator does not want the beneficiary's children to benefit.

These changes are tied to date of death and consequently would have applied to the 200 wills in our sample which were probated in 1989. However, in our sample it is only those wills written from 1983 onwards (114) which might be expected to reflect the changes. If the spirit of the 1982 Act were taken on board, we might expect to see a reduction in the tendency to name a grandchild as a substitute for a child, since the 1982 Act renders such a substitution clause unnecessary.

Table 6.2 compares wills written before and after the 1982 Act took effect. If this legislation were having an effect on will-making, we would expect to find that fewer testators, from 1983 onwards, were naming grandchildren as substitute beneficiaries for their parents (that is, for the testator's children). However, table 6.2 shows that there has been no change and we must therefore conclude that the 1982 Act appears to have had no measurable impact in the expected direction.

The explanation for this would appear to be either caution within the legal profession or a disinclination to amend precedents to remove strictly unnecessary but well-established clauses. It may also be easier for a solicitor to explain to a client the effect of a will if an explicit clause does appear. Unless the pattern in professionally written wills denotes widespread ignorance of the 1982 Act among the legal profession, our finding suggests that both solicitor and testator value the principle of being explicit in naming substitutes, even though this is now unnecessary in law. Substitution, we are arguing, is more than purely a technical consideration.

Finally, in relation to the legal context of substitution, we should indicate that there are particular problems of interpretation here which are more complex than for bequests at first line. This is because there may be differences between the way the testator *intended* to use substitution provisions, and what the legal consequences of the wording of particular clauses would actually be. In coding the content of our wills sample, some of these problems were reproduced. Consider the

TABLE 6.2. *Bequests to testator's child in wills written before and after the 1982 Act*

	Wills written before 31 December 1982 (N = 688)			Wills written on or after 1 January 1983 (N = 114)		
	N	As % of wills from this period	As % of wills from this period which name child	N	As % of wills from this period	As % of wills from this period which name child
No bequest to testator's child(ren)	436	64	—	73	64	—
Includes a bequest to testator's child(ren)	250	36	100	41	36	100
Child(ren) mentioned and substitute provided	120	17	48	19	17	46
Child(ren) mentioned but no substitute	130	19	52	22	19	54

following examples, taken from our sample of wills. In each of these the total estate is bequeathed to the testator's spouse at first line.

Will A

Bequeaths total estate to the testator's wife at first line but adds: ' if my said wife shall not survive me, for such of my sons the said Charles Naylor and Lawrence Naylor as shall survive me and if more than one in equal shares absolutely.'

Will B

At substitution this will states that the estate is to be bequeathed, 'for such of my sons living at the time of my death and if more than one in equal shares, provided that if any son shall die in my lifetime leaving children who attain the age of 21 years such children shall take by substitution and if more than one in equal shares per stirpes the share which the deceased son would have taken if he had survived me.'

Will C

This will also leaves the total estate to the testator's wife at first line with the following instructions about what is to occur in the event of her predecease: 'to divide it equally between my son John Fleetwood and my daughter Elizabeth Jameson.'

In each of these cases the testator has attempted to construct the will so that his or her issue should benefit. But the consequences in practice would be different in each case because of the particular wording, which can be seen if one asks: what would happen if one of the testator's children died before him or herself? In Will A, that share would pass to the testator's surviving child directly, since the will is worded so that the testator's sons substitute for each other, at the second level of substitution. However, Will B would have the effect of passing portions of the estate down the direct line of descent, in the event of predeceases, since the testator's grandchildren are named as substitutes for their own parents at the second level of substitution. In Will B the siblings would only substitute for each other if one had predeceased the testator and had been childless (or if his children had also predeceased), that is, at the third level of substitution. Will C meanwhile does not state what should happen in the event of the testator's children dying first. If this should happen, the testator's grandchildren would in fact stand to benefit under the *per stirpes* rule (discussed above), but the will itself does not state this.

FIG. 6.3. Coding decisions on wills A, B, and C

	Will A	***Will B***	***Will C***
First line	Spouse	Spouse	Spouse
	↓	↓	↓
Substitution: first level	T's children	T's children	T's children
	↓	↓	↓
Substitution: second level	T's surviving child	T's grandchild(ren)	
		↓	
Substitution: third level		T's surviving child(ren)	

Note: T = the testator.

In each of these wills the inheritance outcome is potentially different, and may or may not be what the testator actually intended. We have no way of knowing that. However, in developing our approach to coding and interpreting our sample of wills we have tried not to make assumptions about the testator without firm evidence. We cannot assume a testator's knowledge of the laws relating to substitution. Consequently our coding of the wills is based upon the actual wording of the clauses they contain rather than on a legal interpretation of the consequences of that wording. Hence wills which have wording similar to that of Will C have been coded as having one level of substitution only. Figure 6.3 shows how Wills A, B, and C have been coded.

Who gets named as substitute beneficiaries?

We begin our analysis of the content of substitution clauses by focusing on beneficiaries. Of the 497 wills which include at least one level of substitution, 371 (75 per cent) include named individual beneficiaries and 176 (35 per cent) include group bequests. Some of course include both.

Group bequests in fact are much more frequent at substitution than at first line (table 6.3). Thirty-five per cent of the wills with substitutes include a group bequest at this level, that is, 22 per cent of *all* wills, compared to 6 per cent of all wills at first line. As can be seen from table 6.4, group bequests to grandchildren are popular at all levels. At first line there are 24 cases of a group bequest to grandchildren (50 per cent of first line group bequests). At substitution this rises to 108 cases

TABLE 6.3. *Bequests to groups at first line and at substitution*

N = 800	N	As a % of all wills	As a % of wills with substitution
At least one group bequest at first line	48	6	—
Group bequests at first level of substitution	176	22	35
Group bequests at second level of substitution	102	13	21

(61 per cent of group bequests at substitution). The use of a group bequest to grandchildren at substitution allows a degree of flexibility in that members of the named group not born at the time of writing the will are nevertheless counted as beneficiaries if they are alive at the time of the testator's death. Thus grandchildren born after the will was written (or even after the death of the testator, depending on the terms of the gift) would be included without the need for a codicil or a new will.

TABLE 6.4. *Selected types of group bequest*

	First line (N = 48)		First level of substitution (N = 176)	
	N	As a % of group bequests at first line	N	As a % of group bequests at first level of substitution
Testator's children	15	31	15	9
Testator's grandchildren	24	50	108	61
Testator's great-grandchildren	2	4	5	3
All group bequests	48	100	176	100

The group bequest is therefore particularly well suited to substitution, since by its nature it is intended to cover for future eventualities. It allows a specific gift to be given to people not yet born at the time when the will was written. In interpreting these provisions, the courts have developed 'class closing rules' to facilitate early distribution. These rules also mean that if no-one qualifies as a member of the 'class' named in a group bequest when the testator dies, the class remains open for a limited time until one individual qualifies and then it closes (Miles and Denyer, 1993: 14). It is interesting that female testators, and those who are not married at the time of writing the will, are the most likely to use group bequests at substitution. Though first line group bequests show no significant variation by age or marital status, at substitution both are statistically significant (both at .00 level). This suggests a tendency, in line with patterns identified at first line, for female and unmarried testators to spread their bequests among a wider range of beneficiaries.

How many individual beneficiaries are named as substitutes? Looking at 'first' substitutes only, the number included in the wills ranges from 1 to 23, with a mean of 2.93. If we remove from the analysis the 6 wills which have more than 15 beneficiaries, the mean falls to 2.66 per will. The number of individual relatives (that is, excluding non-kin) per will at substitution ranges from 1 to 8, with a mean of 2.38. When we examine which named individuals are included at substitution, we see patterns which are broadly similar to the ones we identified at first line, in that the overwhelming majority of wills do feature relatives, and blood relatives in particular.

In all, 448 (90 per cent) of wills with substitutes include a bequest to a relative, with 399 (80 per cent) bequeathing to relatives exclusively at substitution (see table 6.5). 'Relatives' here are loosely defined to include blood relatives, step-relatives, and affines. At substitution there is a slightly lower percentage of wills which include a gift to a blood relative, but a slightly higher percentage than at first line bequeath to them exclusively. These differences may be explained by the reduced presence of non-kin and people whose relationship to the testator is not known (see table 6.5).

Which particular individuals are most likely to be named as substitutes? Table 6.6 gives details of the main categories. The most obvious difference between substitutes and first line beneficiaries is that bequests to spouses are rare at substitution. We have only 5 wills

TABLE 6.5. *Presence of, and exclusive bequests to, types of beneficiaries*

	First Line (N = 800)				Substitution (N = 497)					
	Names at least one beneficiary of the type		Bequeaths to this type of beneficiary *exclusively*		Names at least one beneficiary of the type			Bequeaths to this type of beneficiary *exclusively*		
	N	As a % of all wills	N	As a % of all wills	N	As a % of all wills	As a % of wills with substitutes	N	As a % of all wills	As a % of wills with substitutes
Spouse and/ or blood kin	718	89	513	64	409	51	82	328	41	66
Step-kin	16	2	0	0	19	2	4	4	0.5	0.8
Affines	83	10	0	0	61	8	12	16	2	3
Other kin	43	5	5	0.6	24	3	5	2	0.3	0.4
All kin	737	92	577	72	448	56	90	399	50	80
Non-kin	138	17	13	2	31	4	6	8	1	2
Identity of beneficiary unknown	147	18	32	4	80	10	16	35	4	7

which include a spouse at this level.[1] On the other hand, children feature prominently here. If we combine bequests to daughters and sons, 33 per cent of wills with substitutes bequeath exclusively to children (named individually) at substitution, with a further 10 per cent bequeathing to children plus another beneficiary. Only 5 per cent of wills containing substitution clauses bequeath to named grandchildren but, as we have noted, group bequests to grandchildren are common at this level.

After children the most common beneficiaries at substitution are niece/nephews and siblings. Nieces and nephews are the exclusive beneficiaries at substitution in 9 per cent of wills with substitutes and feature in a further 11 per cent along with other beneficiaries. For siblings the corresponding figures are 5 per cent and 10 per cent respectively. Hence when children are named as substitutes they are much more likely to be the sole beneficiaries. This is in contrast with other blood relatives, who are more likely to appear at substitution in wills which combine two or more types of beneficiary.

Affines, who feature in 10 per cent of wills as first line beneficiaries (see table 4.2), are proportionately slightly more numerous at first substitution, appearing in 12 per cent of the wills at this level. Data on individual beneficiaries in our wills indicate these affines are usually the spouse of the first line beneficiary for whom they substitute in 73 per cent of cases. Thus there is a clear pattern of affines acting as 'replacements' for their own spouses at substitution. At first line there are no wills which bequeath to affines exclusively; however, at substitution there are 16 (3 per cent of wills with substitutes). By contrast, fewer non-kin appear at substitution. Only 6 per cent of this group of wills include non-kin, whereas they feature in 17 per cent of wills at first line, though the percentage of wills bequeathing exclusively to non-kin remains static at 2 per cent at first line and at substitution (table 6.5).

As might be expected, it is rare to include ascendant generations in

[1] Two of these wills bequeath the estate to a spouse and a child, or the survivor of them; the third leaves the estate to a daughter, naming the testator's husband as a substitute beneficiary. The fourth will includes various charitable bequests and a cash gift to the testator's wife but leaves the residuary estate to a woman whose relationship to the testator is not clear. The residue passes to the testator's wife in the event of the predecease of that woman. The fifth will in this subset sets up a complicated trust arrangement whereby the testator's wife is to receive a share as a first line beneficiary with the remainder going to a daughter from the testator's first marriage. The testator's wife is then named as a substitute for this daughter.

TABLE 6.6. *Relationship of substitute beneficiary to testator*

N = 497

Relationship of beneficiary to testator	Number of wills which contain substitutes of this type	As a % of wills which include substitutes
Wife	3	0.6
Husband	2	0.4
Daughter	111	22
Son	103	21
Granddaughter	19	4
Grandson	25	5
Great-granddaughter	0	0
Great-grandson	1	0.2
Sister	36	7
Brother	17	3
Niece	51	10
Nephew	48	10
Great-niece	3	0.6
Great-nephew	4	0.8
Aunt	1	0.2
Uncle	1	0.2
Cousin (F)	7	1
Cousin (M)	3	0.6
Mother	1	0.2
Father	0	0
Step-daughter	9	2
Step-son	9	2
Daughter-in-law	14	3
Son-in-law	8	2
Sister-in-law	18	4
Brother-in-law	10	2
Nephew's wife	8	2
Niece's husband	8	2
Friend (F)	10	2
Friend (M)	19	4
Neighbour (F)	6	1
Neighbour (M)	5	1

TABLE 6.7. *Beneficiaries new at substitution*

Relationship of beneficiary to testator	Number of wills which contain substitutes of this type	As a % of wills which include substitutes
Wife	0	0
Husband	1	0.2
Daughter	76	15
Son	67	13
Granddaughter	14	3
Grandson	17	3
Sister	13	3
Brother	5	1
Niece	24	5
Nephew	30	6
Great-niece	2	0.4
Great-nephew	2	0.4
Daughter-in-law	7	1
Son-in-law	5	1
Sister-in-law	14	3
Brother-in-law	7	1
Friend (F)	4	0.8
Friend (M)	2	0.4
Neighbour (F)	1	0.2
Neighbour (M)	1	0.2

Note: these beneficiary types are present in some wills at first line. However, the figures here refer to named individuals who enter the will at substitution only.

wills at substitution, though logically it is quite possible depending on the relative ages of testator and beneficiaries. We have two wills only where this takes place. The first is a home-made will written by a married woman aged 43 at the time the will was written. The testator leaves her entire estate to her husband at first line, but divides it equally between an aunt and an uncle in the event of her husband's predeceasing her. The second will in this category was written by a spinster and was drawn up by a bank. The will includes cash gifts to two of the testator's godchildren with the residue going to the testator's co-resident spinster sister 'in the knowledge that she will look after our mother'. In the event of the sister's predecease the residue estate is to pass to the testator's mother direct.

How far does substitution entail simply rearranging bequests between substitutes who were named at first line, and how far is it used to introduce new beneficiaries to the will?

Three hundred and seventy-two (75 per cent) of the wills with substitution clauses use them to introduce new people to the will (see table 6.1). Table 6.7 gives the details. These beneficiaries cover a wide range including kin and non-kin, though the former outnumber the latter. Indeed it seems that although testators are introducing new people at this level the balance between kin and non-kin does not shift. Predominantly beneficiaries who are new to the will at substitution are the children or spouses of the original beneficiary. Relatives therefore remain the major beneficiaries. However, whilst the overall patterns of bequeathing at substitution reflect those at first line with family taking priority, the substantial numbers of people who are new to the will at this level means that those who stand to benefit here are different individuals, with a broader range of kin represented.

In essence, what is happening at substitution is that gifts intended for the family remain within the family, though passing on to different members. For the most part, the people to whom they pass seem to have been identified by a 'next of kin' logic. However, it is interesting to note that the precise logic operated often differs from intestacy law, and indeed from other aspects of inheritance law, where the law allocates to a *child* the deceased parent's share. When people make wills, they are equally likely to allocate to the surviving *spouse* the share of the deceased husband or wife.

Which beneficiaries are provided with substitutes?

Examining which first line beneficiaries have substitutes named *for* them fills out the picture of how people distinguish between one beneficiary and another in providing substitutes. Table 6.8 shows which types of first line beneficiaries do or do not have a substitute named for them. Table 6.8 implies that when it comes to providing substitutes for beneficiaries, testators distinguish between different types of beneficiary on the grounds of genealogical closeness and, to some extent, on the basis of generation. As might be expected, the testator's closest relatives—spouse and children—are much more likely than other beneficiaries to have a substitute provided. Conversely,

TABLE 6.8. *Wills containing selected categories of first choice beneficiaries who do/do not have a substitute named for them*

Relationship to testator	Number of first line beneficiaries	Provided with a substitute		Provided with no substitute	
		N	%	N	%
Wife	226	156	69	70	31
Husband	68	52	76	16	24
Daughter	196	108	55	90	46
Son	191	108	57	85	45
Granddaughter	46	7	15	40	87
Grandson	54	10	19	45	83
Sister	120	58	48	62	52
Brother	57	25	44	32	56
Niece	99	39	39	69	69
Nephew	87	29	33	61	70
Daughter-in-law	24	3	12	21	88
Son-in-law	12	2	17	10	83
Sister-in-law	29	11	38	18	62
Brother-in-law	20	11	55	9	45
Friend (F)	52	11	21	45	87
Friend (M)	19	4	21	15	79
Neighbour (F)	14	6	21	11	72
Neighbour (M)	8	5	25	6	75

Note: the figures in the second and third columns do not necessarily total those in the first because a beneficiary may have a substitute for one bequest but not another. For example, a daughter may receive an item of jewellery for which no substitute is named and may also receive a share of the residue estate which is covered by a substitution clause. She would therefore feature in both the 'with' and 'without substitute' categories.

substitutes are provided less frequently for grandchildren, who might reasonably be expected to outlive the testator.

The interlocking themes of generation and genealogy are evident also when we examine substitution along the sibling line. Whilst there are marginally fewer siblings with substitutes than without, the pattern of omitting substitutes is more pronounced for niece/nephews. It is also more common for affines not to be covered by a substitution clause. Interestingly, siblings-in-law fare better than children-in-law in this respect. However, the greatest lack of substitutes is evident in non-kin groupings. Three-quarters or more of those wills which name friends and neighbours at first line do not provide substitutes for these beneficiaries. The principle at work here seems to be that the testator's close family should be covered by substitution, whilst other beneficiaries need not be. The naming of substitutes for blood relatives has the effect of keeping assets within the family, especially since the substitute beneficiaries themselves tend also to be blood relatives in the majority of cases.

There is also the question of whether the felt need to provide substitutes varies with the quality of the relationship between the testator and the first line beneficiary. Though this is an issue where the wills data can offer only limited insights, it may be that the naming of substitute beneficiaries implies that a stronger bond (and a continuing obligation) exists, which extends beyond the immediate relationship enjoyed by the testator and first-named beneficiary. In other cases where no substitutes are named, it may be that the testator is quite happy that the gift should be 'lost' because the testator feels no particular obligation beyond the first line beneficiary.

The following will provides an example which illustrates these issues. It concerns the case of a relatively distant first line beneficiary (a niece) who nonetheless has a substitute named for her. It was written by a widow, Elsie Jarvis, who appoints her niece, Helen Baker, and Helen's husband Joe as executors of her estate. Elsie leaves a cash gift to her sister-in-law Mary and the residue to her niece Helen. In the event of Helen's dying first, the residue is to go to Joe absolutely. No substitute is provided for the cash gift to Mary (and in reality it would become part of the residue and therefore pass to the survivor of Helen or Joe). In so far as one can determine this from the will, we assume that this pattern of bequests denotes that the testator enjoys a good relationship with both her niece Helen and the niece's husband Joe, since she has made provision for both of them in her will (though on slightly different terms). Joe benefits directly if his wife dies before her aunt. If his wife survives her aunt, he may of course benefit indirectly through the bequest which passes to her. However, there is an implication that there is a bond sufficiently strong to provide for not only the niece but to ensure that the gift does not lapse if she dies first.

On the other hand, there is no substitute provided for the cash gift to the testator's sister-in-law. Does this result from a difference in the quality of the relationship between the testator and this particular beneficiary? We cannot know the answer to that from the will alone, but it may be so. Equally, it may be important to look at the type of gift involved. This is a cash gift rather than the residue (for which a substitute was provided). In the case of professionally drafted wills it would be deemed neglectful of a solicitor to fail to ensure that there was a substitute for the residue. But the same would not necessarily be true of other gifts. So this raises the question of whether people—either testators or their legal advisers—treat particular *bequests* (not simply particular beneficiaries) differently at substitution. We turn to this issue in the next section.

Forms of substitution

Though there is a sense in which substitution is a single phenomenon, it does take different forms in different wills. Examining these variations—including variations related to the types of bequest involved—tells us more about the models of progression with which people operate when planning the disposition of their property.

One variation concerns the number of progressions which the will allows for, so that even substitute beneficiaries have substitutes named for them in the event of their predeceasing. Though 62 per cent of testators provide for at least one level of substitution, only 29 per cent provide for at least two levels and only 8 per cent for more than two (table 6.9). The maximum number of levels of substitution is five, of which we have only one example.[2] For the most part it appears therefore that testators think only a limited distance into the future when anticipating predeceases. Even then it would appear that they envisage that a disaster scenario (more than one member of the family's dying at the same time) could happen to a married couple but is unlikely, for example, to include three generations of kin.

A second variation concerns the extent to which the introduction of substitutes also changes the ways in which gifts are bequeathed. Two hundred and seventy of the wills (34 per cent) use substitution to

[2] This is contained in a will written by a married man aged 62 who bequeaths his entire estate to his wife at first line. In the event of her predecease the estate is to go to the testator's son, followed by the son's children in the event of his predecease. If the testator's wife, son, and grandchildren all predecease, then the estate is to be divided between the testator's two brothers, or the survivor of them, with the provision that should either brother die leaving a spouse, then that spouse is to take her husband's share.

TABLE 6.9. *Levels of substitution in wills*

N = 800 (all wills) N = 497 (wills with substitutes)

	N	As a % of all wills	As a % of wills including substitutes
One level of substitution only	263	33	52
Two levels only	169	21	34
Three levels only	58	7	12
Four levels only	6	0.8	1
Five levels	1	0.1	0.2

redistribute a gift by splitting it between a larger number and/or a wider range of beneficiaries than was the case at first line (see table 6.1). For example, a total estate which went to the testator's spouse as the first choice beneficiary might be divided between his or her children at substitution. This mechanism for spreading a gift across a wider range of people at substitution occurs in 29% of the first line total estate wills and in 36 per cent of the first line bequests of the residue.

Another way in which substitution is used to extend the range of beneficiaries (and thereby to effect a change in *what* is bequeathed) occurs when a first line gift is split into two or more gifts at substitution. This occurs most commonly in wills which bequeath the total estate at first line and where provision for substitution has the effect of dividing the estate into gifts plus residue. In all, there are 55 wills which introduce new gifts at substitution, of which 40 were total estate wills at first line. In each of these cases the effect is to spread out the estate, and potentially to widen the range of beneficiaries, but without threatening the original gifts made in the will or undermining the position of first choice beneficiaries.

A third variation concerns the issue of whether substitution covers all gifts made at first line, or only certain types of gift. Our sample shows that it is quite common to provide cover for some gifts but not for others. Of the 497 wills with substitution clauses, 275 (55 per cent) cover all first line gifts whilst 222 (45 per cent) provide cover for only a proportion of the first line gifts (see table 6.1).

Thus partial substitution is common in our sample and is linked both to the identity of the first line beneficiary and also to the type of gift. We have already shown that certain beneficiaries (mostly the

FIG. 6.4. Composite wills: cover for selected bequests

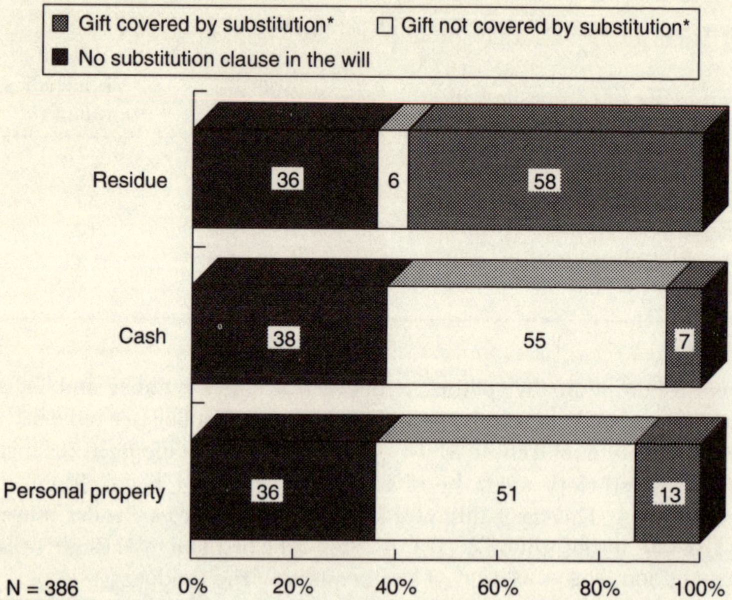

* *Note*: the first two categories refer to those wills which do have some provision for substitution.

testator's close kin) are more likely than others to have substitute beneficiaries named for them. The same applies to certain types of gift. Where testators use partial substitution it is unusual not to provide cover for gifts of total estate and residue. We have only three cases where a testator bequeaths at first line a portion of his or her total estate which is not covered by a named substitute, and only 23 of the 386 wills which include a bequest of residue at first line fail to provide cover for that gift at substitution. As a consequence, bequests of total estate and residue are the gifts which appear most frequently at substitution. By contrast, the majority of first line bequests of cash and personal property are not present at substitution. Only 7 per cent of composite wills which include a cash gift name a substitute for that gift (19 cases out of 288) and only 13 per cent (24 cases out of 192) provide cover for personal property at substitution (see figure 6.4).

Clearly total estate and residue are being treated differently from other types of gift in the provision of substitutes. The fact that these gifts feature in such high numbers in substitution clauses, and indeed are the only gifts appearing in three-quarters of wills at this level, separates them out from other types of bequest. Of course by definition total estate wills which provide substitution must include the gift of total estate (or part of it), there being no other type of gift in these wills. In the case of composite wills, the residue normally would be the most valuable bequest and certainly it would be the bequest which, if not covered by substitution, clearly would leave the will-maker intestate. It is not difficult therefore to understand why substitutions are likely to include the residue. What is much more interesting is to consider why, in composite wills, other types of gifts often are *not* included.

When we pose the question this way round certain types of gift seem to be excluded fairly systematically, whilst others are included. This line of reasoning is supported if we compare partial substitution in professional and home-made wills. As we have already noted (see figure 6.1), over 70 per cent of wills which have been professionally written include substitution clauses whilst only a quarter of home-made wills provide cover for the predecease of first choice beneficiaries. However, there is little difference between professionally drawn wills and those which are home-made when it comes to partial substitution. Forty per cent of professional and 35 per cent of home-made wills omit cover for certain gifts but include it for others (see figure 6.2). Further, the gifts thus omitted are remarkably similar. Table 6.10 shows the comparison for gifts of residue, cash, and personal property. The figures in this table have to be treated with some caution as the number in the 'home-made' column is rather small. Nonetheless it is clear that the two types of will have similar patterns of partial substitution for each type of gift.

So, where partial substitution occurs either in home-made or professional wills, it is cash gifts and personal property which are most likely to be left without substitutes. This pattern suggests that a decision to leave certain types of gift without a substitute should be treated as a meaningful act, not an accidental oversight.

Linking this to the arguments which we have developed in earlier chapters, we would suggest that it relates to the personal and individual elements within wills. In effect, substitutes are not provided for gifts of cash or items of personal property because (in a strong sense) they are specific to the individuals who receive them at first line. In relation to these gifts the point was not so much to find a mechanism for disposing of property, but to use it to honour a specific individual, usually a friend or more distant relative, who would not have a central claim on

TABLE 6.10. *Number of wills which provide no substitutes for selected types of gift × Whether the will is professional or home-made (based on wills which have partial substitution)*

N = 184 (professional), N = 13 (home-made)

	Professional		Home-made	
	N	As a % of professional wills with partial substitution	N	As a % of home-made wills with partial substitution
Residue	21	11	3	23
Cash	150	82	10	77
Personal property	92	50	8	62

Note: the totals of the columns exceed the total number of wills being analysed because certain wills use partial substitution for more than one type of gift.

the estate but who has been a valued person in the testator's life. If that beneficiary dies before the testator, the gift itself loses its meaning. Thus examining different ways in which people use substitution tells us more about what testators are doing when they write wills. We can take this one step further by examining which testators use substitution at all, and who uses it in these different ways.

Who uses partial and full substitution in a will?

Since almost two-thirds of our sample makes use of substitution, it makes sense to ask if there are any characteristics systematically associated with wills where it appears.

It will already be apparent from the discussion in this chapter that the distinction between total estate and composite wills remains important at substitution. Figure 6.5 shows what happens to *bequests* in each of these types of will at substitution. Whilst similar proportions of total estate and composite wills are included amongst those wills which have no substitution at all, there are striking differences when we look at the ways in which each type of will fits into our categories of partial and full substitution. The majority of total estates (213, 52 per cent of all total estate wills) pass as total estate bequests at the first

FIG. 6.5. Bequests at substitution in different types of will

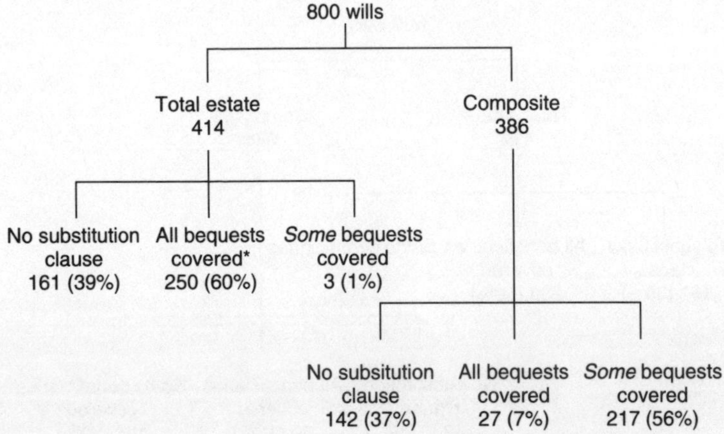

* *Note*: 40% of these get divided into composite wills at substitution (ie bequests plus residue). The remaining 20 pass on as total estate bequests at substitution.

substitution, though about half of these get divided between a greater number of beneficiaries at this level. Typically these are cases where the first choice beneficiary was the testator's spouse. Only 9 per cent of total estate wills get divided into gifts plus residue. In effect, this small number of total estate wills turn into composite wills at substitution. Figure 6.6 shows the cover provided for *beneficiaries* in wills of each type. Only three of our total estate wills failed to provide full cover for all beneficiaries. These are cases where the estate had been divided between more than one person at first line, but only certain of those first choice beneficiaries are provided with substitutes.

Composite wills show a different pattern from total estate wills at substitution. These are wills which had taken a more complex form at first line, including different kinds of gift and normally naming more beneficiaries than do total estate wills. The theme of complexity continues at substitution. Just over half (56 per cent) of the wills which had been composite at first line provide cover only for certain gifts, with a relatively small number (27, 7 per cent of all composite wills) providing substitutes for all gifts. The figures are similar when we look at first choice beneficiaries who are covered by substitution clauses. Fifty per cent of all composite wills include substitution for certain beneficiaries only, with only 13 per cent of composite wills (50 cases) covering all those who receive a bequest at first line. This underscores

FIG. 6.6 Substitution of beneficiaries in different types of will

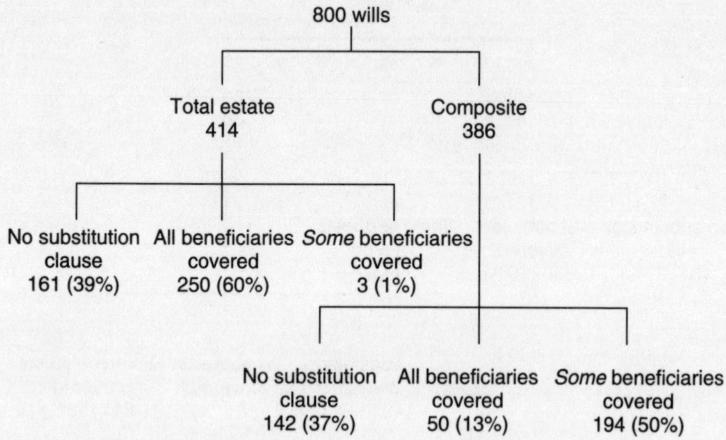

our analysis in chapters 4 and 5 that composite and total estate wills each represent a rather different approach to bequeathing, a pattern which continues into substitution.

Further, the characteristics of testators most likely to write composite and total estate wills are reflected at this level, being linked to the use of partial or full substitution. Estate size clearly bears some relationship to the use of substitution. Figure 6.7 shows that for estates in each quartile there is a greater tendency to include substitute beneficiaries than not, though this tendency is most evident in higher-value estates. However, testators with higher-value estates seem to distinguish between beneficiaries to a greater extent in that they tend to provide substitutes for some beneficiaries only, whereas the majority of wills in the lowest two quartiles provide substitutes for every beneficiary (figure 6.8).

On the surface, it would seem that those with most to leave are less concerned about providing substitution for all their bequests than are testators of more modest means. However, it is quite likely that these differences are a reflection of other characteristics of higher-value wills, noted in chapters 4 and 5: the wider range of beneficiaries which are included, the tendency to spread bequests across a wider range of relatives, and the tendency to include more bequests to non-kin. Since it is generally more distant kin and non-kin who do not have a substitute named for them, we might expect larger-value estates to use partial substitution to a greater extent. This certainly fits with the

FIG. 6.7. Use of substitution × Estate value

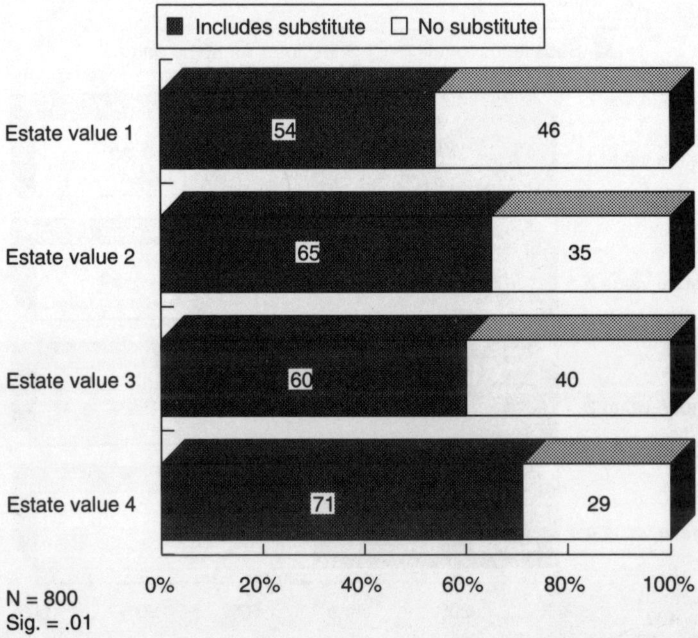

Note: the 'values' in this figure represent the four quartiles of estate values for each sample year, added together. Value 1 is the lowest quartile, value 4 is the highest.

emerging picture that higher-value estates are likely to contain elements of bequeathing which are more individualistic.

A similar conclusion can be drawn about the relationship between the personal characteristics of testators and the use of substitution (see table 6.11). At first sight only marital status is important, whilst the gender and age of the testator have no significance. These latter characteristics show small differences, but neither is statistically significant. Male testators include substitute beneficiaries in their wills more frequently than women testators (65 per cent and 60 per cent respectively), and substitution is more popular with testators over the age of 60 than it is with those under 60 (62 per cent and 56 per cent respectively). However, a different picture emerges when we examine which kind of testators commonly choose to use full, as opposed to partial, substitution (table 6.12). In this instance, a testator's gender, marital status, and age each appear to be relevant factors in determining

FIG. 6.8. Use of partial/full substitution of beneficiaries × Estate value (for wills with substitutes)

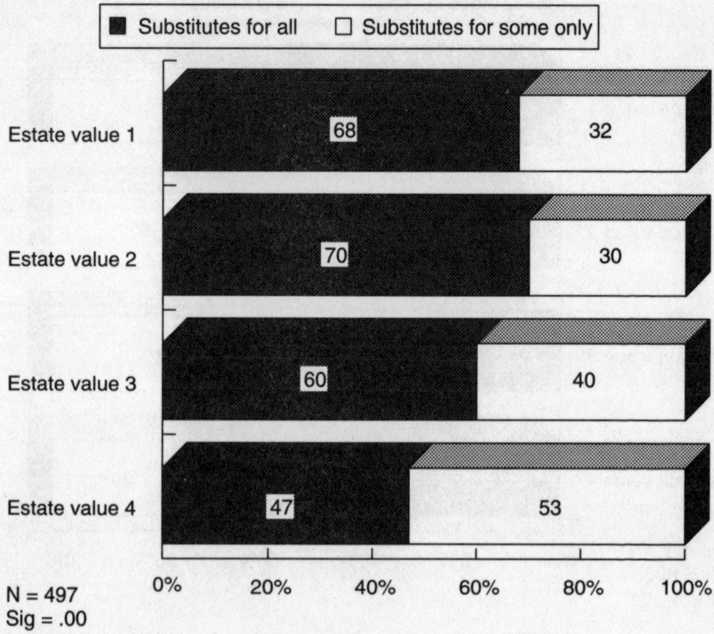

Note: for definition of estate values, see figure 6.7.

the likely *degree* of substitution applied in a will. Male testators provide substitutes for all of their first choice beneficiaries more frequently than do female testators. Full substitution is also favoured by married testators more frequently than by those who were not married when the will was written. In terms of age, testators under the age of 60 use full substitution more frequently than testators who are older. All of these relationships are statistically significant at the .00 level.

If we link this with patterns observed in earlier chapters, partial substitution does begin to look like a strategy adopted by those testators who are including elements in their wills which are personal and individual. It is used precisely by those testators whom we have already identified (on other grounds) as being most likely to include such elements: older people, women who are not married when writing their last will, people with larger estates. This fits with our argument above, based on the type of bequest left without substitutes, that partial substitution arises where there are gifts at first line which are highly

TABLE 6.11. *Use of substitution × Selected testator characteristics*

Gender
N = 800

	Male		Female	
	N	%	N	%
Includes substitutes	248	65	249	60
No substitutes	135	35	168	40
Total	383	100	417	100
Sig. = .14				

Marital status at time of writing will
N = 752 (where marital status could be deduced)

	Married		Single/Widowed/ Divorced	
	N	%	N	%
Includes substitutes	217	73	260	57
No substitutes	79	27	196	43
Total	296	100	456	100
Sig. = .00				

Age at time of writing will
N = 720 (whose ages were known)

	60 and under		Over 60	
	N	%	N	%
Includes substitutes	81	56	356	62
No substitutes	63	44	220	38
Total	144	100	576	100
Sig. = .22				

personal to the individual beneficiary. Full substitution meanwhile may be underscored by a more instrumental logic, being simply a means to avoid the legal complications of intestacy. Alternatively, it may be used by testators who see the process of bequeathing as one in which they are acknowledging responsibilities to people occupying certain 'positions' in relation to themselves, and where they have a responsibility to ensure that the appropriate individuals receive the bequests appropriate to these positions.

TABLE 6.12. *Use of full/partial substitution × Selected testator characteristics (for testators who had included some form of substitution)*

Gender
N = 497

	Male		Female	
	N	%	N	%
Full substitution	171	69	129	52
Part substitution	77	31	120	48
Total	248	100	249	100
Sig. = .00				

Marital Status at time of writing the will
N = 477

	Married		Single/Widowed/ Divorced	
	N	%	N	%
Full substitution	163	75	123	47
Part substitution	54	25	137	53
Total	217	100	260	100
Sig. = .00				

Age at time of writing the will
N = 437

	60 and under		Over 60	
	N	%	N	%
Full substitution	61	75	207	58
Part substitution	20	25	149	42
Total	81	100	356	100
Sig. = .00				

Finally, we should note that there has been some change in the use of substitution clauses over time. Focusing simply upon wills written in the same decade as they were probated, we see a gradual increase in the number of wills which include substitution clauses, both full and partial, and a correspondingly significant downward trend in the

FIG. 6.9. Patterns of substitution provided in wills over time

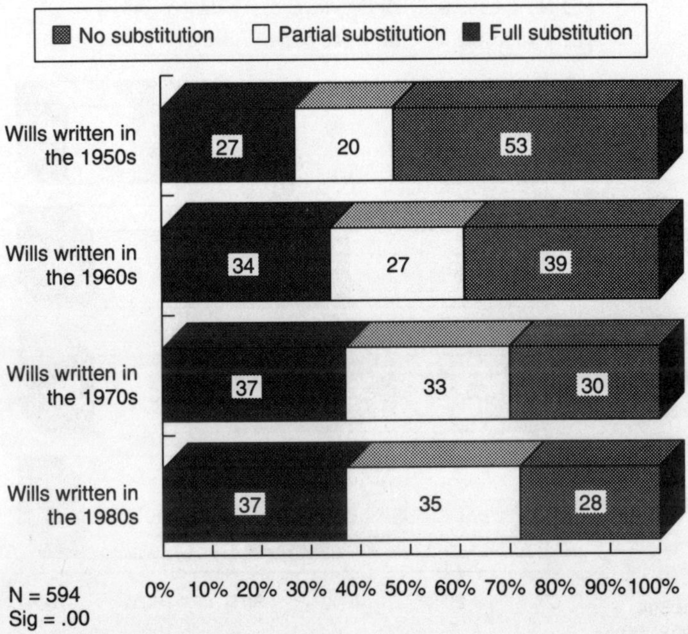

numbers of those without substitution clauses, linked in part to the decline in the proportion of home-made wills (see figure 6.9). There is also an increasing tendency over time to include two or more levels of substitution (see figure 6.10). These tables over-represent will-makers over the age of 75, for reasons explained in chapter 1 which arise from our method of constructing a variable that measures change over time. It is possible therefore that it is elderly testators in particular who have shown an increasing tendency to use substitution. This would also fit perhaps with another line of reasoning, which relates to demographic changes that have occurred in the last forty years, the period covered by our study. As Anderson (1985) notes, it is only from the mid-1970s onwards that the majority of the population have lived to know all of their grandchildren and some of their great-grandchildren. It may be quite simply that wills written by elderly people in our later sample years are reflecting the greater likelihood that the will-makers have lived to see the birth of descendants in the second and third generations and that people are more likely to include a bequest when at least

FIG. 6.10. Levels of substitution provided in wills over time

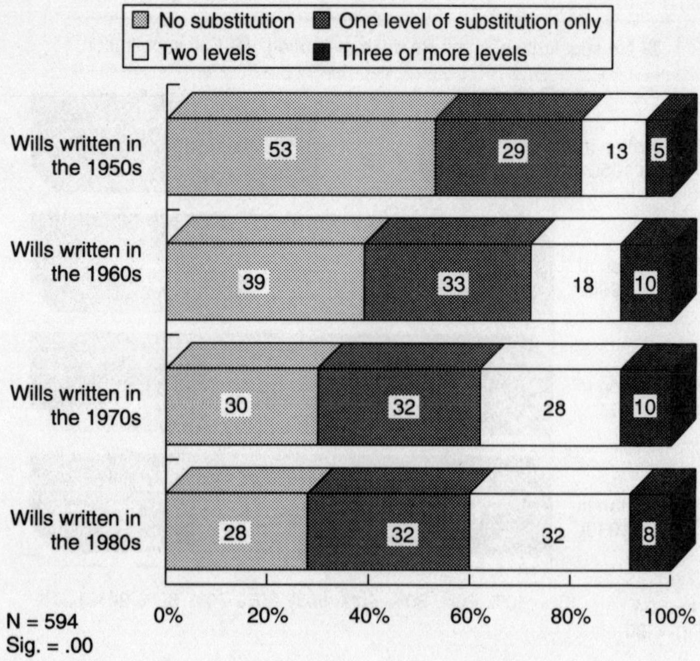

some individuals are known to the testator. Patterns at the first and second levels of substitution would fit with this analysis.

Conclusions

An examination of substitution clauses builds upon our discussion of the data on first line bequests, giving us a further insight into whom the testator counts as important and what items commonly count as inheritable property. The data support the notion of inheritance as a family matter, since first line gifts bequeathed outside the family are absent almost entirely at substitution. In terms of bequests, gifts of total estate and residue are much more likely to be included at substitution than are gifts of cash and personal property.

For most wills, the changes effected at substitution are not dramatic. Although a substantial number of wills use substitution to introduce new people to the will, these new beneficiaries are related to those for whom they cover so that bequests remain within the testator's direct line of descent, or that of siblings. As far as the gifts are concerned, again it is unusual to implement major changes. For the most part, the changes that occur involve different divisions of an existing gift so that it is shared among more people. This may have the effect of altering the actual value of the gift to the individuals receiving it, but in essence the gift itself remains the same. It is those wills which use substitution to introduce new gifts which represent the greatest potential for change, though only a relatively small number do use this strategy. Moreover, the kind of gifts introduced here tend to be cash and personal property, thereby reflecting what happens elsewhere in the will.

We can now add the factor of substitution to the picture of first line bequeathing (discussed in chapters 4 and 5) to construct a more rounded picture of bequeathing patterns in the wills sample as a whole. The picture which emerges is one in which there is a wide variety of patterns of bequeathing from the simplest possible will (total estate, bequeathed only to one beneficiary, no substitutes) to wills which have many complexities built into them (composite, many different beneficiaries, full or partial substitution, differential treatment of beneficiaries). Further, these variations do bear some relationship to the characteristics of testators and the circumstances under which the will was written.

Table 6.13 expresses these variations, through the use of a variable constructed from these various criteria of complexity. The analysis keeps separate total estate and composite wills, and shows how these patterns of complexity vary with certain testator characteristics. This table does not reveal any patterns which are different from those already identified in chapters 4, 5, and 6, but it serves as a useful way of summarising some of the major features of bequeathing patterns. In general, adding in the factor of substitution seems to reinforce rather than to cut across patterns identified in first line bequests. The people who write the most complex wills when substitution is added to the equation tend to be the same groups whom we identified as most likely to write composite rather than total estate wills: women, older testators, people who are not married at the time of writing their last will, testators with estates in the highest quartile of value. Yet it is also evident from table 6.13 that the likelihood of writing a simple or a complex will is not related to testator characteristics in any straightforward way. For example, if we compare the most complex total estate wills (category 5) with the most complex composite

TABLE 6.13. *Patterns of complexity in bequeathing × Selected testator characteristics*

Type of will	Gender				Marital Status				Age				Estate Value			
	Men		Women		Married		Divorced		Up to 60		Over 75		Lowest quartile		Highest quartile	
	N	%	N	%	N	%	N	%	N	%	N	%	N	%	N	%
1. Total estate, single beneficiary, no substitution	71	(55)	56	(44)	53	(46)	62	(54)	49	(42)	19	(16)	40	(32)	17	(13)
2. Total estate, 2+ beneficiaries, no substitution	11	(32)	23	(68)	2	(7)	28	(93)	2	(6)	16	(52)	17	(50)	4	(12)
3. Total estate, single beneficiary, with substitution	96	(66)	49	(33)	109	(80)	27	(20)	34	(26)	27	(21)	36	(25)	27	(19)
4. Total estate, 2+ beneficiaries, with substitution	19	(38)	31	(62)	1	(2)	45	(98)	10	(22)	16	(36)	16	(32)	6	(12)
5. Total estate, 2+ beneficiaries with substitution, one or more 'complications'	33	(57)	25	(43)	37	(65)	20	(35)	11	(21)	19	(36)	14	(24)	14	(24)
6. Composite, no substitution	53	(37)	89	(63)	24	(19)	106	(81)	12	(10)	66	(49)	35	(25)	38	(27)
7. Composite, with substitution	13	(57)	10	(43)	11	(48)	12	(52)	4	(20)	6	(30)	3	(13)	10	(44)
8. Composite, with substitution, one 'complication'	57	(43)	76	(57)	36	(28)	91	(72)	11	(10)	57	(52)	24	(18)	44	(33)
9. Composite, with substitution, two or more 'complications'	30	(34)	58	(66)	23	(26)	65	(74)	11	(14)	33	(43)	15	(17)	40	(46)
Total	383	(48)	417	(52)	296	(39)	456	(61)	144	(20)	259	(36)	200	(25)	200	(25)

Note: (i) 'Complications' are differential treatment of beneficiaries anywhere in the will; partial rather than full substitution; new bequests introduced at substitution; (ii) Categories 1, 2, 3, 4, 6, and 7 have *no* 'complications'; (iii) Categories 6, 7, 8, and 9 have any number of beneficiaries.

wills (category 9), there is substantial variation in the testator characteristics associated with each. The same is true if we compare the simplest total estate wills (categories 1 and 2) with the simplest composite ones (categories 6 and 7). It would seem that the two types of will do represent different ways of bequeathing, and that to some extent testator characteristics operate differently within each type of will.

Therefore from the perspective of our analysis as a whole, the most important feature of patterns of substitution identified here is that they lend support to our argument that there are two different frameworks of meaning associated with bequeathing, and that these are linked with two different types of will, total estate and composite. Our final chapter discusses the implications of this.

7 Families, Bequeathing, and the Law

In previous chapters we have examined key patterns of bequeathing in our sample of wills, and explored the often complex implications of these for the nature of will-making in Britain over the last four decades. In this chapter we build upon these basic patterns and themes, but focus directly on what they suggest about the relationships between property and family/kinship.

We approach this broad issue from two different directions. To begin with, we examine what the wills tell us about family and kinship in the context of property transmission, by examining configurations of family and kin as beneficiaries in wills, and the salience of property in this context. In particular, we develop the concept of 'inheritance families' to structure our ideas in this section. Secondly, we go on to explore what the wills tell us about property in the context of family and kinship, by asking whether the patterns and types of bequeathing we have observed are suggestive of the perpetuation of 'inheritable' property. In broad terms, therefore, we are shifting the level of analysis away from what the patterns of bequeathing are, and towards a focus on what they express about family and property and how they express it.

However, in order to understand the significance of this we need to consider the relevance of the medium—wills—through which such expressions are made. In the final section, therefore, we return to questions about the simultaneously public and private dimensions of wills, and examine their capacity not only to express relationships between family/kin and property, but potentially also to constitute and authenticate those relationships as part of a wider formal legal discourse. In doing this, we return to the key questions about the interplay between bequeathing and the law with which we began this book.

Constructing 'inheritance' families in wills

We have already noted that the picture of formal bequeathing which we have built up is one where family and kinship predominate. As we have seen, taking our four sample years together, 92 per cent of testators name at least one relative as a first choice beneficiary, with spouses and blood relatives predominating over others. Seventy-two per cent bequeath only to kin, with this figure reaching a strikingly high 89 per cent in what we have called total estate wills. Testators with small estates were particularly likely to focus exclusively on kin (77 per cent of testators in the lowest quartile estate size over the four sample years). Furthermore, it is not only as first choice beneficiaries that family members predominate, but we have also shown that blood relatives, especially those in the direct line of descent of the original beneficiaries, are those most commonly named as substitute beneficiaries. These patterns have remained stable over our four sample years. Broadly these findings are in line with earlier studies (Horsman, 1978; Diamond Commission, 1977; Hamnett, Harmer and Williams, 1991), though as we have indicated these other studies have focused on the identity of the 'main beneficiary' whereas our study indicates that formal bequeathing is handled as a distinctively family matter even when the full range of beneficiaries and substitute beneficiaries is taken into account. There is, therefore, no doubt that formal bequeathing is treated as a family matter and has continued to be so treated, in the face of far-reaching social and economic change, since the 1950s when our own study begins.

However, we can go further than this by trying to understand what the patterns of formal bequeathing we have identified express about testators' family relationships. One way to approach this is to ask whether wills appear to activate ideas about what a family is for inheritance purposes. Can we identify a common model of an 'inheritance family' across our data set, from the many specific inheritance families constructed by individual testators in their wills?

If we scan our data for such an inheritance family, the answer to the question has to be no, because the images of family which testators present in their wills are too variable to fit straightforwardly into a uniform version. Nevertheless, we can trace patterns in the ways in which wills activate ideas about inheritance families. We have argued in previous chapters that it is possible to identify general principles about family relationships in patterns of formal bequeathing which apply broadly to our data set over the four sample years. These principles centre on the three overlapping categories of generation, genealogical position and 'next of kin'. Thus what type and size of gift beneficiaries receive, and on what terms, will depend upon their generational and genealogical position in relation to the testator, and upon whether or not they appear, amongst all beneficiaries named, to be defined as the testator's 'next of kin'. These categories work in an explanatory way for our data only if we see them as overlapping: thus the pattern of bequeathing identified in any one will is likely to be the product of a mixture of the three.

Although they do not produce a uniform picture of an inheritance family, these principles suggest some of the broad ways in which testators conceptualize family and kinship for the purposes of formal inheritance and, in particular, demonstrate that testators place a premium on genealogical and generational closeness in their wills. However, these principles are not the whole story, and we can get further in our search for an inheritance family if we examine other key features of our data set. Specifically, we want to build on some of the arguments of previous chapters to suggest that instead of looking for a uniform end-product—a standardized inheritance family—we should instead search for patterns in the ways in which testators construct their own inheritance families in their wills. If we place the construct*ing* rather than the construct*ion* at centre stage in this way, then some important patterns begin to emerge. There are two key and interrelated dimensions to the constructing of inheritance families in wills. The first concerns ways in which family and kin are positioned as beneficiaries, and the second refers to mechanisms for the passing on of property.

Positioning family and kin as beneficiaries

We are not going to reiterate here our detailed analysis of patterns of 'who gets what' in wills, but instead we will pull together and develop points we have made earlier in the discussion. We shall build on our observation that there appear to be two distinct frameworks of meaning associated with bequeathing to family and kin, and link this to the argument that there are different ways in which individuals can be 'positioned' as beneficiaries.

We shall call the first way of positioning kin 'ascriptive'. Testators who position their family and kin ascriptively in their wills are those who appear to be using the genealogical status of their beneficiaries as the key positioning principle. The logic by which their beneficiaries are organised and differentiated in the will is one which is fixed to the genealogical positions those beneficiaries occupy in relation to the testator, rather than being contingent upon other aspects of the relationship which the testator has with each of them. Thus ascriptive positioning entails treating beneficiaries of the same kin type in exactly the same way. It is most likely to involve leaving unconditional bequests—since imposing conditions entails introducing an alternative logic—or bequests which impose identical conditions on all beneficiaries sharing any one genealogical position in relation to the testator.

If we define ascriptive positioning in this way, our data show that it is most commonly applied to categories of kin which are in a direct line of descent from the testator, namely children and grandchildren. Ascriptive positioning is also characteristic of wills which bequeath everything to a single beneficiary who is apparently 'next of kin', most commonly the testator's spouse. Furthermore, it is the form of positioning most likely to be used throughout a will in which a spouse or members of the direct descent line are present as beneficiaries.

What does this tell us about the way in which wills are being used? It suggests that testators who position their beneficiaries ascriptively may well be expressing a model of testamentary responsibility based on kin types. Though of course we cannot know what was in the mind of these testators when they wrote their wills, the pattern observed suggests that the role of the will for these testators is to execute a set of clear-cut responsibilities to kin based upon ascriptive genealogical position. Such a version of responsibilities may also imply a mirror image of rights, so that people in certain genealogical categories in relation to the testator are deemed to have a right to an inheritance, and those outside these categories have no formal rights.

The second form of positioning of family and kin is what we are calling 'relational' positioning. Testators who use this form of positioning in their wills are those who appear to be acknowledging the individuality of some of their family and kin relationships, most obviously by treating beneficiaries of the same kin types in different ways. As discussed earlier, this can involve bequeathing unequally to people of the same kin type, or bequeathing differentially—for example giving different specified items of personal property to beneficiaries of the same kin type—in ways which may or may not be unequal and hierarchical in terms of the relative economic or symbolic value of the gifts. Relational positioning appears to involve a logic of organising and differentiating family and kin based on factors to do with the specificity or individuality of particular relationships. It is, therefore, more likely than ascriptive positioning to produce bequests which are conditional in ways tied in to the life circumstances of the beneficiaries.

In our data, relational positioning is most commonly applied to categories of kin which are not in a direct descent line to the testator, and in particular to siblings, nieces, and nephews. It is least likely to be applied to children and grandchildren. Where this does happen, characteristically each member of the kin type receives a different item of personal property in a way which simultaneously acknowledges individuality in relationships without obviously ranking them in terms of economic value. Relational positioning is particularly characteristic of wills in which the beneficiary who is apparently being treated as the testator's closest or 'next of kin' falls outside the direct line of descent, for example a sibling, niece or nephew. More generally, it is characteristic of wills where no spouse–beneficiary is present.

By comparison with ascriptive positioning, the more variable and flexible approach to the inclusion and treatment of beneficiaries here suggests that these testators have a weak notion of the rights of certain specified kin to inherit or of their own responsibilities to pass on property straightforwardly to them, and a strong notion of testamentary freedom. However, in some senses, this is tempered by the general tendency to treat spouses and children (where present) more favourably than other kin, and by the common pattern of differential (rather than obviously unequal) bequeathing within a kin type which involves giving different items of personal property to all members of that type. In some senses, this latter form of differential bequeathing may both support the notion of equality within a kin type whilst also recognising the individuality of particular relationships. The exercise of freedom here is not in whether to bequeath, but how to do it.

Mechanisms for bequeathing

The two forms of positioning of family and kin which we have identified suggest that the constructing of 'inheritance families' is a fairly complex and subtle business. However, we need to add yet another layer of complexity to the analysis. This concerns the mechanisms for bequeathing which are used in the wills. We shall show that it is only in an examination of the interplay between these mechanisms and the two forms of positioning that we can begin to understand the processes of constructing inheritance families.

In earlier chapters we have identified two alternative mechanisms used to pass on property in wills. The first is characteristic of what we have called 'total estate wills', and the second of 'composite wills'. We shall discuss the significance of each in turn.

First, there is the mechanism of total estate bequeathing, where a testator simply passes over all his or her property as an undifferentiated whole. The implication is, that after death, everything which the testator owns will be added together and passed either to one beneficiary or to more than one in the proportions the testator specifies in his or her will. These proportions may or may not be equal.

Fifty-two per cent of wills in our sample used the total estate bequeathing mechanism for first line bequests, and of those 'total estate' wills which contained substitution clauses the majority (51 per cent) used the same mechanism for substitute beneficiaries. The majority of total estate wills (60 per cent) did contain full substitution clauses, demonstrating, on the whole, that these testators were attempting to ensure that their total estate would pass to substitute beneficiaries, should the first choices predecease the testator. In total, 250 wills, 31 per cent of our sample, were total estate wills with full substitution clauses. There is a sense therefore in which testators using total estate bequeathing were expressing a desire, or perhaps a responsibility, to pass on their whole estate tidily and unequivocally.

Although in principle total estate bequeathing can be accompanied by relational positioning of family and kin—for example a total estate can be bequeathed in unequal proportions to more than one beneficiary of the same kin type—in practice this was rare. Empirically therefore total estate bequeathing and ascriptive positioning of family and kin were closely aligned in our data set. It looks therefore as if we can identify a distinctive group of total estate bequeathers who acknowledge a responsibility to pass on their whole estates tidily and unequivocally to a tightly construed group of family and kin, usually spouses and/or kin in the direct line of descent.

As we noted in chapter 4, it is not possible to identify one single type of testator who uses this kind of bequeathing, but our data suggest that it is characteristic of married testators, whether male or female, who commonly use it as a vehicle for passing a total estate to a spouse, and of male testators (more of whom are married at the time of writing their last will than are women testators). As a whole, testators who bequeath total estate are younger than those who bequeath in a composite way, and are more likely either to have written their wills at least 10 years before their death or not to have revised them during that time. We have suggested that wills of this type written by younger people may simply be seen as safety nets to provide for circumstances which the testators do not really believe—or wish to believe—will occur in the near future, namely their own deaths.

The second mechanism used to pass on property in wills is what we have called composite bequeathing. This involves making specific bequests of particular items or types of property, rather than simply adding the whole lot together and passing it on as a total estate. This can be done in a variety of ways, including dividing the bulk of an estate—for example, by bequeathing a house, a business, liquid and non-liquid assets—or simply making a number of bequests of cash or personal property and then bequeathing the residue as a whole to one beneficiary or, in proportions, to more than one. In practice the distinction between these two forms of composite bequeathing is blurred, since it is not always possible to tell what proportion of an estate is represented by a specific gift such as a house or a business and so on. Similarly, unless they are straightforward bequests of sums of cash, it is not usually possible to discern whether or not the differential gifts made through composite bequeathing are equivalent in economic and symbolic value. However, it is sometimes possible to spot obvious economic inequalities.

Composite bequeathing characterised 48 per cent of our wills sample at first line, although some of these wills reverted to total estate bequeathing in substitution clauses. However, a more substantial proportion of composite than total estate wills either did not contain substitution clauses or contained clauses which gave only partial coverage. In contrast to total estate bequeathers therefore, composite bequeathers seem less concerned with the tidy and efficient transmission of their whole estate, and more concerned with making links between the specificity of certain items or types of property on the one hand, and certain individual members of their family or kin group on the other. Our data suggest that composite bequeathing is characteristic of older testators, who are more often female and widowed. Their wills are more often written less than 10 years before their death, and are therefore more 'up to date' than those of testators who use total estate bequeathing. In a sense, we think this points to the use of composite bequeathing and relational positioning of beneficiaries as part of a 'life review' conducted in old age by testators who are genuinely anticipating their own death, and wishing to acknowledge a fairly wide range of relationships which may have been established over many years.

What begins to emerge therefore is a set of empirical links between ways of positioning family and kin as beneficiaries on the one hand, and mechanisms for passing on property on the other. In principle these links are not prerequisites of each of the categories, but in practice they are clearly linked in our data set, so that testators who deploy ascriptive positioning of family and kin are much more likely to use total estate bequeathing, and those who deploy relational positioning are more likely to use composite bequeathing.

We have separated out these principles of bequeathing and positioning to demonstrate what testators are doing when they construct their inheritance families, and how they are doing it. However, we should reiterate that these construct*ing* principles do not straightforwardly represent types of will or construct*ions* of inheritance family which can be represented in a typology.

For example, in terms of the form in which wills are written at first line, the two mechanisms for bequeathing—total estate and composite—can be separated clearly, but in other senses the boundaries between these two, and between ways of positioning family and kin, are not neat. Especially when we draw substitution clauses into the picture, what emerges is something more like a continuum of complexity within the wills sample, rather than an easy typology of wills (see table 6.13, and the discussion of complexity in bequeathing in chapter 6). At one extreme, there are the simplest wills in our sample. These include those which bequeath total estate at first line and end there, with no provision for substitutes. Moving further along the continuum, we would find total estate wills which provide substitute beneficiaries for every gift, followed by those which provide partial substitution for the total estate. At the other extreme, the most complicated wills in our sample would be those which contain a combination of different bequests at first line, only some of which are covered by substitution, and where this is further complicated by the presence of several layers of substitution. In between fall those wills which are simple at first line but complex at substitution, such as those which begin as total estate wills but are then divided up if the first choice beneficiaries predecease.

We recognise, therefore, that the distinction between total estate and composite wills is not absolute, although the analytical distinction between these as forms of bequeathing is clear. Similarly, if our unit of analysis is the will, then the distinction between ways of positioning family and kin is not absolute, because different positioning principles can apply at the different levels of the same will. However, we have been able to demonstrate how principles of bequeathing and of positioning of family and kin are most commonly applied in tandem, in ways which are clearly activating distinctive interpretations of the inheritance family.

Constructing inheritable property in wills

In exploring the ways in which testators construct inheritance families in their wills, we examined both the positioning of family and kin as beneficiaries, and forms of bequeathing. We demonstrated that a full understanding of the constructing of inheritance families requires that we engage with the use of property in wills, as well as the appearance of family and kin as beneficiaries. In this section we want to approach these issues from the other direction, and ask what the patterns of bequeathing which we have observed tell us about property in the inheritance process. Essentially we are asking how testators seem to treat different types of property, rather than its formal status in law. Do testators treat certain types of property as 'inheritable' in the sense that the property itself is singled out for transmission?

There are potentially many ways to approach this, but for the purposes of this discussion we want to ask whether it is possible to identify a 'currency' of inheritable property in wills. To begin with, we need to ask what such a currency might look like. At its simplest level, the currency might be defined on the basis of the criterion of suitability. We would expect to be able to identify as inheritable those forms of property which are treated as though they are particularly suitable or appropriate for transmission in wills. Using this criterion, inheritable property would, therefore, be property which appears most commonly in wills.

However, we think that the criterion of suitability or appropriateness of property for transmission through formal inheritance is only one dimension of the currency of 'inheritable property' we are seeking to identify. We need to add to it the criterion of preservation: the idea that 'inheritable property' means forms of property which testators attempt to preserve as the inheritance process unfolds. In the English legal context there are two key ways of preserving property in this sense. The first is to include substitution clauses in a will, which specify what is to happen to a particular gift in the event of a first choice beneficiary predeceasing the testator. The second is to use a trust and to create life interests. This effectively allows a beneficiary use of or benefit from the property during his or her lifetime only, and the testator then makes provision for what is to happen to it after the beneficiary's death. These two mechanisms of course achieve different ends, but their significance here is that they both represent ways of preserving or tagging a particular gift in the process of inheritance in a way which suggests that it is the property that matters, not just the beneficiary.

Using this two-stage definition, suitability and preservation, can we identify property with these inheritable characteristics in the wills? If we begin by looking again at the types of property which appear most frequently in wills, and then go on to apply our preservation criterion, the results initially look rather unpromising. For example, total estate bequeathing, which characterises 52 per cent of the wills at first line, seems to suggest that many testators are not distinguishing *any* items of inheritable property from the bulk of their estates. Wills which are characterised by composite bequeathing at first line (48 per cent of the sample) are more promising, given that they include specified bequests, although one-third of these simply make cash gifts and then bequeath the residue.

Specified bequests of general personal property (of a variety of types) other than cash do appear in 50 per cent of the composite wills (24 per cent of the total wills sample). However, if this says anything about inheritable property, it is that only a minority of testators identify a wide range of items as inheritable. This explanation is weakened, however, when we employ our preservation criterion. Eighty-seven per cent of all personal property bequests are not covered at substitution, and only 5 per cent are subject to a life interest, and this suggests that the property in itself is not being accorded an inheritable character, as we have defined it.

Other specified gifts are made only in small minorities of wills, but one of these is worth mentioning here. Eleven per cent of wills include a specific gift of a house. Of course, as we argued in chapter 4, in many cases total estate bequests are likely to include houses although they do not specify them individually and, where the total estate passes to one person, it is perhaps possible that any house which is included in this is being regarded informally as inheritable property. However, in these cases, the will is not being used to tag or identify a house specifically as inheritable property in its own right.

It may also be the case that a house has a special status if it has been the testator's home and s/he wishes to preserve it as a home for close relatives to occupy. Of the houses specified in wills, 33 per cent of these gifts are subject to a life interest. The relatively high proportion of these gifts which apply this preservation criterion suggests that, for a small number of testators at least, houses do represent inheritable property. The life interest would allow a current occupant to remain in the house, even under certain conditions to sell it and reinvest the money, whilst at the same time determining the ultimate destination of the property. In wills which have these provisions, a house is being treated as inheritable property in a very strong sense.

So far then we have a picture where there appears to be no single currency of inheritable property in wills, although our data suggest that minorities of testators do accord certain types of personal property, and houses, inheritable status (in the sense in which we are using the term). How might we explain the apparent failure of testators to treat their property in ways which imbue it with inheritable character in their wills? One possible explanation is that inheritable property does not exist in any meaningful sense at all, and that is why we do not see it reflected in wills. However, we cannot conclude from a study of wills alone, without exploring the wider and more informal aspects of inheritance process, whether or not this is the case.

Alternatively, it is possible that inheritable property does exist 'outside' of wills, but that the law and the practice of professional advisers conspire against its perpetuation through the medium of wills. In some senses, our data do seem to support this explanation. So, for example, the legal costs involved in using a trust to create a lifetime interest may be prohibitive, and our interviews with professional advisers suggest that they are likely to discourage this practice, except for substantial assets (Masson, 1994). Similarly, objects and items other than houses may be specified and given to particular individuals informally, either completely outside of the mechanism of a will or within wills, but invisibly, as part of a total estate or residuary bequest. We have noted that the input of professionals into will-making is likely to discourage the inclusion of specified items in a will, suggesting that wills as a data source are likely to under-represent people's desire to specify bequests in this way. However, on the other hand, it is also the case that wills drafted by a professional are more likely to be composite in nature than are home-made wills (50 per cent of solicitor-drafted wills are composite, as compared with 40 per cent of home-made wills). This suggests that people who wish to bequeath in a composite manner may be particularly likely to go to a professional for help and, although some may subsequently be dissuaded from doing this, the resulting pattern of composite bequests may not be such an underestimate of people's desire to bequeath in this way as originally suggested.

We think a more satisfactory explanation emerges when we begin to review the fundamental conceptual question of what it is we expect to see when we look for inheritable property. The discussion so far has drawn on the assumption that inheritable property, if it exists, takes the form of items or things which exist meaningfully outside the will and the legal process, and get specified or referred to in the will. Intuitively the idea of inheritable property suggests an object or objects which get imbued with particular meaning, and this conceptualization is indeed one which has been applied in anthropological work (for example, Weiner, 1992). The role of the law, and of professionals, as we have discussed it so far, is simply one of facilitating this process, or of constraining it.

However, this approach overlooks the possibility that wills actually *construct* forms of inheritable property which do not exist meaningfully outside or beyond this formal mechanism of bequeathing. Once we accept this possibility, this sheds new light on the two major categories of 'total estate' and 'residue', which previously we have excluded from our discussion of inheritable property. In essence, we suggest, these types of bequest also get constituted (not merely communicated) through wills.

We can explain this best by introducing the idea that the distinctiveness of total estate or residue bequests lies in the *formal gesture* as well as the practical act of bequeathing which the will constitutes. The formal gesture that a bequest of total estate in a will represents is something like 'a gift of everything I own' to one or more beneficiaries, and a bequest of the residue represents 'a gift of the rest of everything I own'. These formal gestures are produced in an interaction between testators as actors and the legal process. Therefore they cannot be understood as a product of ideas which people have in their heads which simply get translated into bequests in wills, nor can they be understood as a direct consequence of legal regulation. Instead, they become constituted through the process of making a will, which includes combinations of: testators' bequeathing intentions, the law and precedents governing inheritance and intestacy, the role of professionals, and the nature of wills as public and private documents. The interaction of these elements, which gives us the key to understanding the character and construction of inheritable property, also has a wider relevance for our analysis of the role of the law in will-making, and we shall therefore briefly consider each element in turn.

We begin with testators' bequeathing intentions. These should not be understood as though they exist in isolation from the legal and cultural context of inheritance, but neither should they be seen as straightforward products of these contexts. Figure 7.1 suggests some ways in which we might understand the position of testators as actors, engaging or interfacing with the law in the production of total estate and residue bequests as inheritable property. Though of course the analysis of data from wills gives us no direct access to the intentions and motivations of testators, the point about figure 7.1 is that a range of different meanings is possible within the formal gesture of making a will. Through their interactions with the law, testators may produce forms of will which look very similar to each other, but which actually represent attempts by different testators to express different meanings which each associates with the act of bequeathing.

The second element is the law and precedents governing inheritance and intestacy. The law governing inheritance has tended to be more concerned with the form of wills than their content, although intestacy law clearly concerns itself with the ways in which estates are divided and distributed. Any will must take a prescribed form if it is to be treated as valid under the law (see chapter 3). Because all our wills had been proved, they all had been accepted as valid and therefore did conform to the form of will required by the law. More interestingly, however, most of the sample betray the influence of legal processes, and especially the input of the legal profession, over and above the strict requirements of the law. Most were written in a form based on legal precedents (the nature of which we discussed in chapter 3). This applies even to many of the wills which were home-made, especially if they were clearly based on purchased will-making kits or advice books, indicating that the writing of these types of wills was not entirely outside the influence or prescriptions of the law. However, our data show that about four-fifths of wills in the four sample years were drawn up by professionals, and that this proportion has increased over time, rising to around 88 per cent for wills made since the 1960s. So the input both of the law itself and of the legal profession is quite extensive in respect of the form which wills take. Although the law does not dictate, for example, who should receive total estate or residuary gifts in wills, what it does do is to make them available as part of a formal

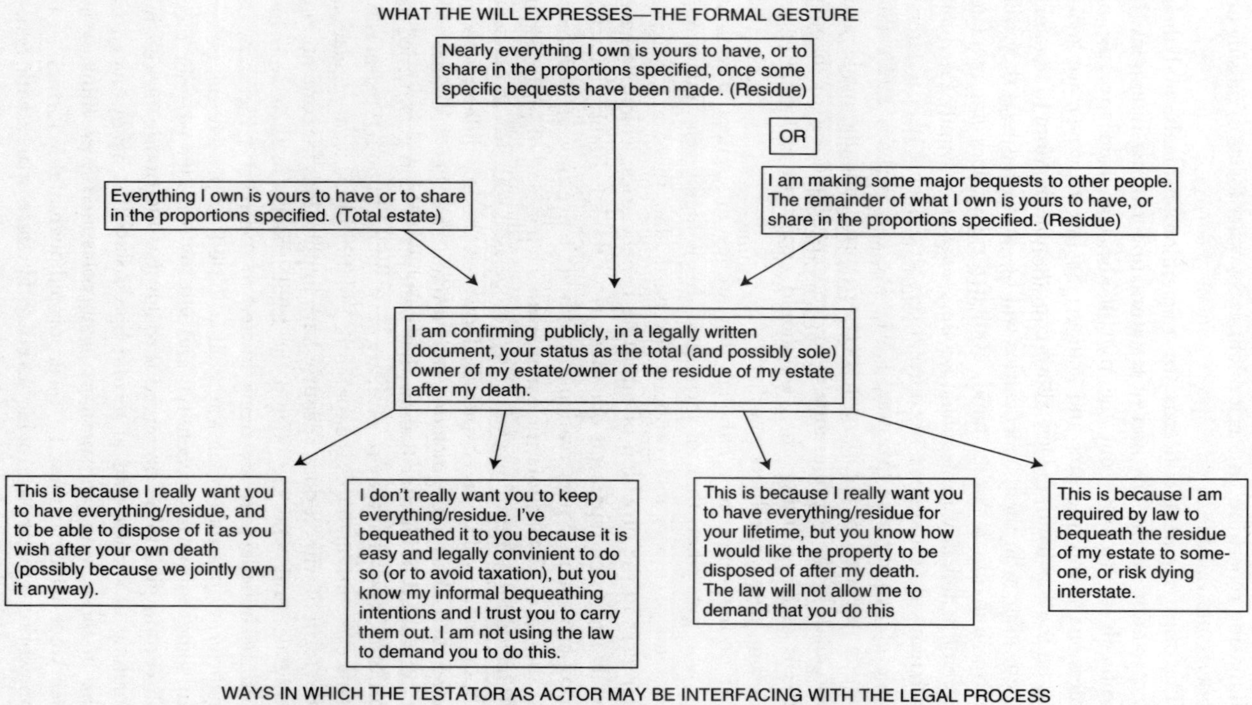

FIG. 7.1. Testator intentions and the interface with the law

will-making repertoire, just as it might make other forms of passing on property unavailable.

The third element concerns the role of professionals, and their interpretation of the law and of testators' bequeathing intentions. It is difficult to separate out the role of the law from the role of professionals who interpret and activate the law. However, we know that, on the one hand, the law allows considerable freedom to testators to determine who their beneficiaries will be, and what gifts they will receive. But, on the other hand, even if the law does not regulate choice of beneficiary, professional advisers—aware of Family Provision legislation—do sometimes, of course, exert an influence over testators' choice of beneficiaries (Masson, 1994). We can perhaps tackle this question through a comparison between professionally made and home-made wills. If professionals' advice were significant in shaping patterns of bequeathing, then we should expect to find differences between these two subsets of wills.

We do find differences, although they are less differences of content (e.g. who gets what) than of form, and this is highly relevant to our discussion of inheritable property. In particular, there are striking differences in the provision of substitute beneficiaries, which we have already suggested represents one measure of the inheritable character of property, namely preservation in the inheritance process. It is here that the input of solicitors is clearest, with 71 per cent of professional wills including substitution clauses, by comparison with just 25 per cent of home-made wills (see chapter 6). However, the key difference is in *whether* such clauses are included rather than *what* they say, since the data discussed in chapter 6 show that patterns of who gets named as substitutes, and what they receive, are very similar in both types of will.

However, although this is apparently a matter of the legal regulation of the form of wills, it does of course have implications for content. Put simply, testators who are offered the legal 'spaces' in their wills for substitute beneficiaries are being invited to construct a hierarchy of beneficiaries in a particular way (that is, based on predecease, rather than some notion of perpetuity), and also to consider whether they wish certain gifts to be preserved through the inheritance process by remaining as specific gifts at second line. As well as being invited to think in these ways (and perhaps being prevented from thinking in other ways which cannot be incorporated within this formal legal framework), testators are being asked to fill these spaces with beneficiaries. Whether or not individual professionals take it upon themselves to suggest who these beneficiaries might be, we can see that their existence as formal beneficiaries is at least in part produced by, and within, a formal legal discourse of inheritance.

The final element in the production of 'formal gestures' concerns the nature of wills as public and private documents. Wills are a social and cultural form of expression as well as prescriptions for bequeathing practice. The form which wills take, and their nature as documents which are peculiarly both public and intimately private, are key elements in the analysis of formal bequeathing. It is perfectly reasonable to suppose that testators use (not necessarily strategically) the formal legal status of wills in particular ways to achieve ends which are not wholly material. So, for example, it is in this context that we should view the symbolic significance of making a gift of 'everything' in a public, formal, legal way. In practice, as we have suggested, testators who do this may have differing ideas about what actually should happen to their property in terms of material distributions, and all kinds of informal negotiations may take place outside the will. Indeed the testator may have created a 'secret trust' which requires a beneficiary to pass the property to others whose identities are not disclosed in the public will. Of course we cannot explore this in a study of wills alone. The point here is that the very formality and legality of wills is likely to be highly significant in the inheritance process, but needs to be read as something with which people interface in a variety of ways.

A final example will help us to make this point more clearly. In chapter 6, we discussed the issue of the naming of grandchildren as substitute beneficiaries. We noted that, counter-intuitively, there has been a slight increase in this practice even though it is no longer a legal requirement. Had testators, and professional advisers, simply followed the law in order to achieve the appropriate material ends, then we would have expected to see a decrease in such naming. Although there are various possible explanations for this, as we indicated in chapter 6, it is perfectly plausible to argue that the presence of grandchildren as named substitute beneficiaries in wills serves a symbolic as well as material purpose in the context of testators' family relationships.

It is worth restating that we cannot regard wills—which are simultaneously, and possibly uniquely, public and private documents—as a straightforward window onto family responsibilities and relationships. Wills are inherently *formal* documents, and we understand very little about the processes through which people come to use and express formality in their kin relationships. We know that the form of wills is heavily influenced by solicitors and professionals, by guidelines for will making, by the current legal regulation of inheritance and intestacy. But we know less about how and why people make use of the formality of wills in their informal family lives.

Our discussion of inheritable property has suggested that, as a consequence of the interaction between the four elements of the will-making process we have identified, 'total estate' and 'residue' bequests are constituted as inheritable property in wills. Of all gifts in our wills sample, they display most clearly and unequivocally the two features of inheritable property we identified earlier: *suitability* for inheritance (they are the most commonly cited gifts in our sample) and *preservation* in the inheritance process (they are the gifts most often preserved through substitution and the use of life interests).

The more general point that this helps us to make about the relationship between the law and bequeathing is that this is a complex relationship. We have tried to move beyond the idea that law and bequeathing are separate entities which may influence each other, and to lay appropriate emphasis on the formal, public, documentary aspects of the process. However, we have also argued for a view of testators as actors, engaging with the social and legal context in the production both of their individual wills and of a wider discourse of formal bequeathing. It is in the light of this approach that we want finally to return to one of the key themes of this book.

Wills, testamentary freedom and the law

Our discussion of inheritable property has brought questions about the nature of wills as public and private documents, and about the formal legal process through which they are constructed, back into focus. As we have argued, a written will is the product of a process through which testators' concepts of family and of property, and of the relationship between the two, are constituted and authenticated as part of a formal legal discourse. So, in this final section of the book, we will draw together the different strands in our study concerned with the interplay between bequeathing and the law, around one of the key themes underpinning our study: that of testamentary freedom.

In our discussion in chapter 3, we indicated that, though testamentary freedom remains an important principle, the law relating to inheritance, intestacy, and related issues does make certain assumptions about the claims to an estate of certain individuals who are related to the testator. We argued that, during the course of the twentieth century, these assumptions have crystallized around three principles: that any economic dependants should continue to be supported from the testator's estate; that, for other kin, genealogical closeness in the blood line should govern the strength of claims; and an increasing expectation that the claims of a surviving spouse should take precedence over all others. Our discussion here will focus on how far bequeathing behaviour reflects the same principles.

We can deal very briefly with the issue of economic dependants, since our wills data have very little to tell us about this issue, except in relation to spouses with whom we deal separately. Probated wills by definition are last wills, and our data show that normally these are made in old age (see chapter 3). It would be unusual therefore for testators to have young children at the time of writing a last will, a fact confirmed by the finding that our wills contain very few guardianship clauses. There is very little in our wills data which could be interpreted as provision for any other economic dependants, though of course we cannot exclude the possibility that such provisions are being made without being so specified. A gift of life interest in a house may well be to protect a dependant, for example.

In relation to our other two issues—the claims of those who are close in the blood line and of spouses—our wills do reveal some interesting patterns. It is useful to link these to the issue which is debated in legal texts, namely that testamentary freedom can be allowed to continue in English law because in practice testators do acknowledge the claims of close kin; if they ceased to do so, it is argued, the law would need to step in to protect those interests (see chapter 2). Do our wills provide any evidence that this remains the case or, conversely, any clues that testators are departing from acknowledging the claims of close kin and exercising their testamentary freedom by bequeathing in more individual ways?

The overriding message of our wills data is that kin are privileged over non-kin, and predominate as beneficiaries. We have shown the extent to which this is the case in this and earlier chapters, and have identified the three overlapping principles of generation, genealogical position and 'next of kin', which operate to favour beneficiaries' kin who are genealogically and generationally close, both at first line and in substitution clauses. Spouses and children, in particular, are favoured and—in line with what the law assumes—if there is a surviving spouse s/he is very likely to be bequeathed the total estate, or most of the estate. Therefore spouses and children are the most frequent recipients of the two key types of inheritable property we have identified: total estate (most commonly bequeathed to spouses) and residue (most commonly bequeathed to children). Our data certainly do not give any indication of a widespread move towards disinheriting close kin in these categories.

Does this mean that English testators, through their exercise of testamentary freedom, do protect the interests and rights of those kin whom the law assumes should be so protected? Whilst on the one hand the overwhelming tendency of English testators to bequeath to their kin, and to favour their close kin, does suggest this, on the other hand our earlier observations about the ways in which people bequeath, and construct their inheritance families, points towards some disparity between the idea of rights and interests of kin on the one hand, and bequeathing behaviour on the other. Specifically, we want to return briefly to our discussion of the distinction between ascriptive and relational positioning of kin to make this point.

Arguably, ascriptive positioning of beneficiaries—which apparently is based upon the genealogical position of the beneficiary in relation to the testator—is the closest it is possible to get in the framework and discourse of wills to expressing the idea that certain categories of kin should inherit as of right, and that their interests should be protected through inheritance. We have seen that this is particularly characteristic of our total estate wills, and is a frequently used mechanism for bequeathing to a surviving spouse. Relational positioning, however, which appears to be based upon an acknowledgement of the individuality of specific relationships, does not evoke the idea of rights and interests of kin emanating from their kin positions in quite the same way. In other words, it is based on a different set of principles which may, or may not, have the effect of privileging close kin as beneficiaries in wills.

It would be too simplistic to suggest that relational positioning encapsulates the idea of testamentary freedom, whereas ascriptive positioning does not, not least in the light of our arguments about the complex interrelationship between testators and the law, and the aspects of the legal process which form the context in which the testator as actor operates. In that sense, the whole concept of testamentary freedom is perhaps open to question. However, relational positioning does seem to operate on the basis of principles of bequeathing other than those given expression in Family Provision and

Inheritance law. For example, the idea that the genealogical relationship between the parties alone, or the existence of a relationship of economic dependence between them, should govern judgements about choice of beneficiary and type of gift, does not find clear expression in those wills which display relational positioning.

Our data demonstrate that there are certain circumstances in which wills using this type of positioning of beneficiaries are likely to be written; in particular, they are written by testators who, when they write their last will, are not married and are closer to death than the average for our sample. In particular, female widows and spinsters seem more likely to write this type of will which acknowledges a wider range of relationships and which does so on a more individual basis. In this type of will, though most gifts are still kept within the family, it is a 'family' defined in a broader sense.

The messages about testamentary freedom and its expression are mixed, therefore. On the one hand, we find no evidence of a widespread disinclination to favour those categories of kin which the law assumes testators to have some responsibility for, and the position of surviving spouses seems particularly strong. On the other hand, we do see the operation of principles which seem contrary to the idea that genealogical position or economic dependence confer inheritance rights. Ironically, perhaps, bequeathing behaviour in relation to spouses reinforces other legal processes which mean increasingly that it is surviving spouses—usually women—or people who have never been married, who are those most likely to find themselves in a position where relational positioning, and the exercise of a more radical testamentary freedom, may seem a real possibility.

Bibliography

Abel-Smith, B., Zander, M. and Brooke, R. (1973), *Legal Problems and the Citizen*, London, Heinemann.

Anderson, M. (1985), 'The Emergence of the Modern Life Cycle', *Social History*, 10, 69–87.

Bailey, S. (1967), *Law of Wills*, sixth edition, London, Pitman.

Bryman, A. and Cramer, D. (1990), *Quantitative Data Analysis for Social Scientists*, London, Routledge.

Clark, J. B. (1988), *Parry and Clark The Law of Succession*, ninth edition, London, Sweet and Maxwell.

Comyn, J. and Johnson, R. (1970), *Wills and Intestacies*, Oxford, Pergamon.

Crane, F. R. (1957), 'Family Settlements and Succession' in F. R. Crane and R. H. Graveson, *A Century of Family Law 1857–1957*, London, Sweet and Maxwell, 227–55.

Cretney, S. M. (1975), 'Reform of Intestacy—the best we can do', III *Law Quarterly Review*, 77, 95.

Cretney, J. and Masson, J. (1990), *Principles of Family Law*, London, Sweet and Maxwell.

Dainow, J. (1940), 'Limitations on Testamentary Freedom in England', 25 *Cornell Law Quarterly*, 337.

Davey, M. (1988), 'Testamentary Promises', 92 *Legal Studies* 92.

Davidoff, L. and Hall, C. (1987), *Family Fortunes: Men and Women of the English Middle Class 1780–1850*, London, Hutchinson.

Davies, D. T. (1983), *Will Precedent and Capital Transfer Tax*, second edition, London, Butterworths.

Denning, T. (1980), *The Due Process of Law*, London, Butterworths.

Diamond Commission (1977), *Royal Commission on the Distribution of Income and Wealth*, Cmnd 6999.

Eekelaar, J. and Maclean, M. (1986), *Maintenance After Divorce*, Oxford, Oxford University Press.

Engels, F. (1985), *The Origin of the Family, Private Property and the State*, Harmondsworth, Penguin. (First published in 1884.)

Fellows, M., Simon, R., and Rau, W. (1978), 'Public Attitudes about Property Distribution at Death and Intestate Succession Laws in the United States', *American Bar Foundation Research Journal*, 321–91.

Finch, J. (1989), *Family Obligations and Social Change*, Cambridge, Polity Press.

Finch, J. and Hayes, L. (1994), 'Inheritance, houses and the concept of the home', *Sociology*, 28, No 2, 417–33.

Finch, J. and Hayes, L. (1995, forthcoming), 'Gender, inheritance and women as testators', in S. Lyon and L. Morris (eds.), *Gender Relations in Public and Private: Changing Research Perspectives*, London, Macmillan.

Finch, J. and Mason, J. (1993), *Negotiating Family Responsibilities*, London, Routledge.

Finch, J., Mason, J., Hayes, L., and Wallis, L. (forthcoming), *Inheritance, Property and Family Relationships*, London, UCL Press.

Finch, J. and Wallis, L. (1993), 'Death, inheritance and the life course', in D. Clark (ed.) *The Sociology of Death: Sociological Review Monograph*, Oxford, Blackwell, 50–68.

Friedman, L. M. (1966), 'The Law of the Living, the Law of the Dead: Property Succession and Society', *Wisconsin Law Review*, 340–78.

George, E. and George, J. (1964), *Brighouses Short Forms of Wills*, eighth edition, London, Sweet and Maxwell.

Government Actuary (1991), *Eighth Survey of Occupational Pension Schemes*, London, HMSO.

Hamnett, C. and Mullins, B. (1992), 'Housing inheritance and equity extraction by elderly home owners and intergenerational wealth transfer', paper presented to the conference on *Past, Current and Future Initiatives on Ageing*, London: Economic and Social Research Council.

Hamnett, C., Harmer, M., and Williams, P. (1991), *Safe As Houses: Housing Inheritance in Britain*, London, Paul Chapman.

Harbury, C. (1962), 'Inheritance and the distribution of personal wealth in Britain', *Economic Journal* 72, 854–68.

Harbury, C. and Hitchens, D. (1979), *Inheritance and Wealth Inequality in Britain*, London, Allen and Unwin.

Horsman, E. G. (1975), 'Avoidance of Estate Duty by Inter Vivos Gifts', *Economic Journal*, 85, 516–30.

Horsman, E. G. (1978), *Inheritance in England and Wales: the evidence provided by wills*, Oxford Economic Papers No 30, NS, 409–23.

Inland Revenue (1980), *Capital Transfer Tax and Settled Property*, London.

Inland Revenue (1988), *Discretionary Trusts a Research Study*, London.

Justice (1971), *Home Made Wills*, London, Charles Knight and Company.

Kahn Freund, O. (1955), 'Matrimonial Property Law in England', in W. Friedmann, *Matrimonial Property Law*, Toronto, Toronto University School of Law, Comparative Law Series No 2, 267–314.

Kendig, H. L. (1984) 'Housing tenure and generation equity', *Ageing and Society*, 4, 3, 249–72.

Kiernan, K. (1989), 'The family: formation and fission', in H. Joshi (ed.), *The Changing Population of Britain*, Oxford, Blackwell, 27–41.

Langbein, J. (1975), 'Substantial Compliance with the Wills Act', 88 *Harvard Law Review* 531.

Law Commission (1973), *First Report on Family Property: A New Approach* (H.C.P. 274).

Law Commission (1974), *Second Report on Family Property: Family Provision on Death* (H.C.P. 324).

Law Commission (1989), *Family Law Distribution on Intestacy*, (H.C.P. 60).

Law Commission (1993a), *The Effect of Divorce on Wills*, Cmnd 2322, London, HMSO.

Law Commission (1993b), *The Law of Trusts*, Law Commission Consultation Paper No 133, London, HMSO.

Law Reform Committee (1973), *Interpretation of Wills*, 19th Report, Cmnd 5301.

Law Reform Committee (1980), *Report on the Making and Revocation of Wills*, 22nd Report, Cmnd 7902.

Leather, P. (1990), 'The potential of home equity release in old age', *Housing Studies*, 5, No 1, 3–13.

Macfarlane, A. (1978), *The Origins of English Individualism: the Family, Property and Social Transition*, Oxford, Blackwell.

Masson, J. (1994), 'Making Wills, Making Clients', *The Conveyancer*, 267–74; 360–9.

Mellows, A. R. (1983), *The Law of Succession*, London, Butterworths.

Miles, G. and Denyer, P. (1993), *Wills: Probate and Administration*, Oxford, Blackstone Press.

Miller, J. G. (1977), *The Machinery of Succession*, Oxford, Professional Books.

Miller, J. G. (1993), 'Reform of Intestate Succession', in A. Bainham and D. Pearl, *Frontiers of Family Law*, London, Wiley.

Moffat, G. and Chesterman, M. (1988), *Trust Law Text and Materials*, London, Weidenfeld and Nicolson.

Morton Report (1951), *Report of the Committee on the Law of Intestate Succession* Cmnd 8310, London, HMSO.

Munro, M. (1988), 'Housing Wealth and Inheritance', *Journal of Social Policy*, 17(4), 417–36.

Naresh, S. (1980), 'Dependant's Application Under the Inheritance (Provison for Family and Dependents) Act 1975', 96 *Law Quarterly Review* 534.

Pahl, J. (1989), *Money and Marriage*, Basingstoke, Macmillan.

Platt, J. (1981), 'Evidence and Proof in Documentary Research', *Sociological Review*, 29, 1, 31–66.

Pettitt, D. (1978), *The Will Draftman's Handbook*, London, Oyez.

Robson, J. (1938), 'Freedom of Testation', 1 *Modern Law Review*, 297–307.

Russell Committee (1966), *Report of the Committee on the Law of Succession in Relation to Illegitimate Persons*, Cmnd 3051, London, HMSO.

Scott, J. (1982), *The Upper Classes: Property and Privilege in Britain*, London, Macmillan.

Scott, J. (1990), *A Matter of Record: Documentary Sources in Social Research*, Cambridge, Polity Press.

Shaffer, T. (1970), *Death Property and Lawyers*, New York, Dunellen.

Simes, L. (1954), *Public Policy and the Dead Hand*, Ann Arbor, University of Michigan Press.

Simpson, A. (1986), *A History of the Land Law*, Oxford, Oxford University Press.

Todd, J. and Jones, L. (1972), *Matrimonial Property*, London, HMSO.

Townsend, P. and Davidson, N. (eds.) (1982), *Inequalities in Health: the Black Report*, Harmondsworth, Penguin.

Tyler, E. (1971), *Family Provision*, London, Butterworths.

Weiner, A. (1992), *Inalienable Possessions: The Paradox of Keeping-While-Giving*, Berkeley and Los Angeles, University of California Press.

Which? (1991), *Wills and Probate*, London, Hodder and Stoughton.

Whitehouse, C. and Stuart-Buttle, E. (1990), *Revenue Law*, eighth edition, London, Butterworths.

Index